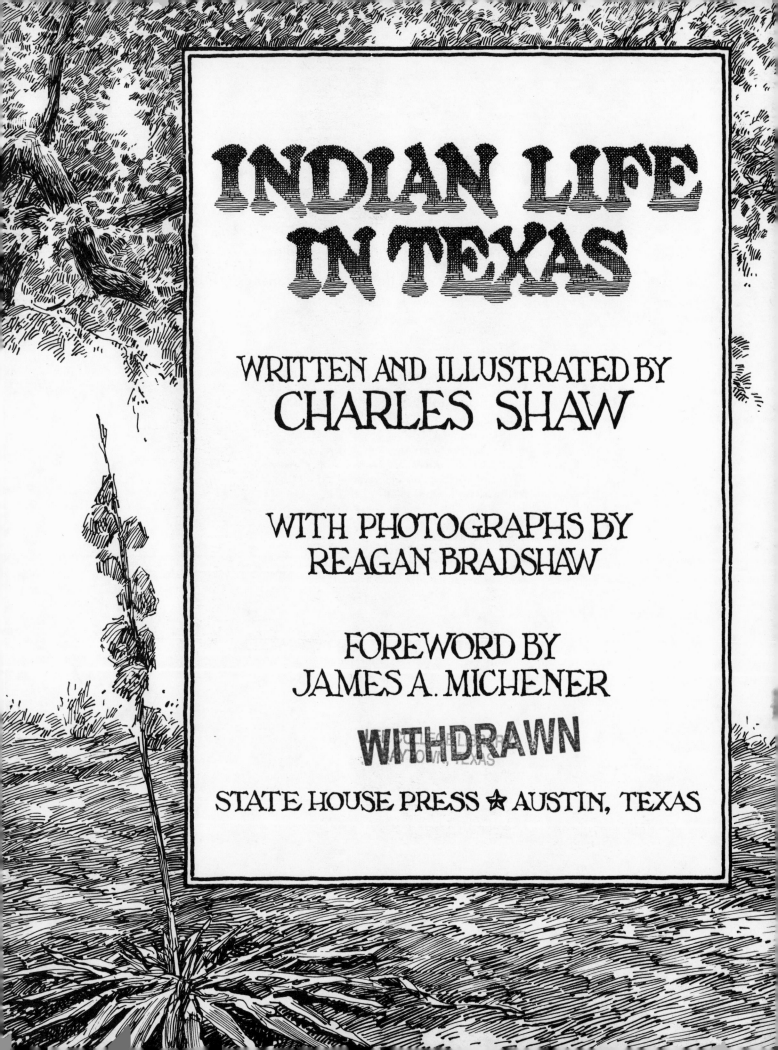

INDIAN LIFE IN TEXAS

WRITTEN AND ILLUSTRATED BY
CHARLES SHAW

WITH PHOTOGRAPHS BY
REAGAN BRADSHAW

FOREWORD BY
JAMES A. MICHENER

STATE HOUSE PRESS ★ AUSTIN, TEXAS

First Edition

Library of Congress Cataloging-in-Publication Data

Shaw, Charles, 1941–
   Indian Life in Texas.
   Bibliography: p.
   1. Indians of North America—Texas—History.
2. Indians of North America—Texas—Pictorial works.
3. Texas—Description and travel—1981– —Views.
I. Bradshaw, Reagan, 1943– . II. Title.
E78.T4S45 1987   976.4′00497   87–17950
ISBN 0-938349-20-1
ISBN 0-938349-21-X (pbk.)

For Sam and Mary
and
Alex and Mildred

TABLE OF CONTENTS

ACKNOWLEDGEMENTS

First of all to Tom Munnerlyn and Debbie Brothers, owners of State House Press, who kept the faith in a first book author. My thanks to Michaele Haynes and Carol Canty who shared their considerable expertise so freely. To Raymond Apodaca, executive director of the Texas Indian Commission, for cheering us on and making the photo section possible—paving the way and providing assistance whenever we needed it.

Thanks also to Joe Sierra of El Paso and Mike Pedraza, Tribal Council Governor of the Tigua Indians; Nelson Celestine of the Alabama-Coushatta; Frank McLemore and Greg Gomez of Dallas, and Michael Suke and Lyla Sailors of the Texas Band of Kickapoo Reservation in Eagle Pass.

We all stand on the shoulders of those who went before us. The broad shoulders that hold me up belong to Mickey Thurgood, who taught me to draw—among many other useful lessons.

And my everlasting affection to Gay Shaw, who has kept her own brand of faith even when I could see no reason to.

FOREWORD

It was with considerable interest that I learned of Charles Shaw's book on the Indians of Texas. No person that I know would be better qualified to produce this type of treatment, because Shaw has three qualifications which would be difficult to equal.

First, he is a superb illustrator, master of a delicate pencil, a genius in laying out a page or a spread or an insert in which his drawings will appear, and possessor of a unique style for indicating movement, tension, bold action and whole-body reaction to a situation. Through years of hard work with the pencil and brush he has honed his skills until they respond to whatever task they face. He creates splendid pictures.

Second, he has considerable skill in organizing his pages so that action and emotion blend. His night scenes are haunting; when his horses gallop across the plains they are real horses and real plains. He is an expert on costumes, equipment and accoutrements of a period so that his work acquires a valuable sense of verisimilitude. They are good history and a helpful accompaniment to written texts.

Third, Shaw is a master of Texas history, the outdoor type, the conduct of the Rangers, the behavior of Indians, the look and feel of wagons and frontier stations and remote barns and houses. His pencil is ideally attuned to the depiction of Texas at various periods of its history, and he is the perfect artist to have done this book.

I speak so warmly of Shaw because I worked with him over a period of more than a year when he was illustrating one of my books. When to my great satisfaction that book won a T. R. Fehrenbach award, I knew it was because of his drawings and not my words. We had enjoyed an association of mutual profit, one I shall always look back upon with delight.

The present book is more than just a series of fine drawings depicting Indians. It explains to the reader four historical stages through which Indians of Texas passed and shows some of the differences that characterized the periods. It reminds the reader, especially the Texan reader, of the importance of Indian life in his region in the old days, and it forces him to reflect upon the fact that the white settlers of Texas ultimately expelled the Indian almost totally and sometimes brutally from his state. Texas was the only western American state to do this, and the trivial little reservation group of the Alabama-Coushatta that were allowed to remain at a site near Woodville is minimal compared to the vast reservations like those in nearby New Mexico or the distant Dakotas.

To see most of the descendants of the Indians who once occupied Texas one must go to Oklahoma, but in the fourth section of the book the photographic essay by Reagan Bradshaw makes amends, so that the reader can catch a glimpse of what contemporary Texas Indians are like. They are, as Shaw's vigorous sketches prove, the inheritors of a noble tradition.

When I worked on the materials covered so well by this book, I gained the conviction that the Indian periods of Texas prehistory and history were among the most interesting, colorful and challenging of all the dramatic periods of this state's remarkable history. The Texas Indians could be violent when they had to be, cruel when faced by resolute white opponents, but also well disciplined and reliable partners when treated well. It's refreshing to me to see once again depictions of what they were like, for they were a unique group of people well worth remembering.

JAMES A. MICHENER
AUSTIN, TEXAS

AUTHOR'S INTRODUCTION

This book shows what it was like to be an Indian in early Texas. My intention is to capture the flavor and to evoke the feel of the life led by the people who lived in our state before us. To achieve this end, neither paragraphs of description nor photographs of relics left behind is adequate. Therefore, I've chosen to use an art form called "illustrated narrative." The stories that follow are drawn from my imagination, but everything shown in the pictures and every event described in the narrative is based on archaeological and historical fact. The result is not so much a book about Indians as it is a book about people who happen to be Indians.

The experience of the American Indian in Texas can be divided into four distinct segments or eras. Of the first three eras each is shorter and more violent than the one preceeding. The fourth era—the twentieth century—is still unfolding.

First came centuries of Prehistory, which began with the migration of the Asian hunter-gatherers across the Bering land bridge into the New World. Over a period of tens of thousands of years, virtually every corner of the western hemisphere became home to some descendants of these first wayfarers, and by the time the last ice age ended and the rising oceans submerged the land bridge, the American Indian was here. For our purposes, this first epoch lasted until the Indian discovered wild European horses escaped from Spanish herds and decided to ride them, in the Spanish manner, rather than eat them, as their ancestors had done with the small native horses that had once wandered the grasslands.

The second era in the history of Texas Indians began with the nomadic tribes on horseback, early in the seventeenth century. Learning horsemanship from the Spaniards (in spite of Spanish attempts to prevent Indians from coming into contact with horses), Indians in what was then northern Mexico learned to ride; and this skill, along with the horse itself, spread northward. As the Spaniards expected, they did indeed rue the day the Indian learned to ride. From about 1650 to just after 1700, mounted Lipan Apaches ruled this part of the world. The Lipans, however, were but pale forerunners of what was to follow. Comanches began to visit Texas, and finding the pickings good, called on their relatives to join them. This was the Golden Age of the horse Indians in Texas. For 250 years, they were a powerful force in Spanish and Mexican Texas. Along with the few white residents of Texas, the horse Indians dominated the weaker Indian tribes.

The end of this era came with Mexican General Santa Anna's loss to the Texas army at San Jacinto on April 21, 1836. With the independence of Texas came a flood of Anglo immigrants bent on making a new life for themselves and their families. This new life was centered on agriculture and the cultivation of the land. Acreage on which Indians had lived and hunted for generations was now to be turned over by the white settler's plow. Except for the fleeting time Sam Houston spent in charge of Texas' policy toward the Indian, the governments of Texas wanted the Indian to just disappear, and if he wouldn't oblige voluntarily, then the Anglo leadership would see him destroyed where he stood. The state did just that, with a fifty-year assault aimed at eliminating all Indians from Texas.

The story of the last era is still being written today. Although Texas has three Indian reservations—the Alabama-Coushatta at Woodville in East Texas, the Kickapoo near Eagle Pass on the Rio Grande, and the Tigua in El Paso—there are more native Americans living off the reservations than on them in the state. The 1980 census reports Texas as ninth in total Indian population with a count of 40,074. This figure compares with South Dakota's 45,101 and Oklahoma's 169,464. Even with over 169,000 Indians in residence, the old Indian Territory is in second place numerically. California has 201,311 Indians living within its borders.

To show the American Indian in Texas today, I have enlisted the help of my friend Reagan Bradshaw. An eminently sensitive man and consummate craftsman, Reagan has produced the photo essay that comprises the fourth and final part of this book. He has spent many hours photographing Indians in Texas, telling their story in exceptional style. His work sums up graphically what Indian life in Texas is today.

Charles Shaw

BOOK ONE . . . PREHISTORY

"In the beginning there was nothing but Darkness, Water and Cyclone. All the Hactcin, who were Supernaturals and personifications of the power of all objects and natural forces, were here from the beginning. They made the world first, and then the sky. The earth was made in the form of a living woman and called Mother. The Sky was made in the form of a living man and called Father. He faced down and she faced up. They were the mother and father of the Jicarilla."

Origin myth of the Jicarilla Apache
as told by T. E. Mails in *The People
Called Apache,* Prentice-Hall, 1974

Man arrived in the western hemisphere during the Pleistocene Era, an age that lasted 60,000 to 75,000 years and ended about 7,000 years ago. During this period, better known as the Ice Age, a large portion of the earth was covered with glaciers which held so much of the world's water that the levels of the seas were some 200 feet below what they are today. This meant that many land masses which are now under shallow water were then dry land. The Bering Straits where man crossed over from Asia to the New World was such a spot, and the new land in which he found himself is now called Alaska.

At that time Alaska's climate was very different from what it is today. Because of a shift in the positions of the earth's magnetic poles, the area that we now call the arctic, although by no means tropical, was quite temperate and tolerant of human habitation.

Man didn't come to the America's for the purpose of conquest. These ancient hunter-gatherers were only following herds of game animals. In so doing, they unwittingly migrated, populating new territories as their numbers grew. On at least three occasions, the glaciers melted and receded enough to create natural pathways out of Alaska to the south and east. The animals followed these trails and the people came behind them.

Both animals and man came out of the glacier fields at about the present northern boundary of the United States. It is little wonder that the people continued south into a land teeming with game of every description, laced with rivers of clean water, and graced with endless forests and rolling grasslands. It must have seemed like heaven to a people just removed from the tundra and table-top flatness on the other side of the ice.

By 1,200 B.C., in the lowland jungles of the Mexican Gulf Coast, descendants of these simple foragers had created a civilization that we call the Olmec. Some scholars believe them to have been the forefathers of the Mayans. The Olmecs were able to build a civilization here because they had free time to devote to civilized activities. Elsewhere in the New World, people were kept busy trying merely to sustain life. Here, the environment provided food with little human effort, so man was able to proliferate and specialize. He could take the time to create art and music, to form political systems, and to look out at the universe and make calendars by which to plant his crops.

The Olmec, the Maya, and later the Aztec, once established in Central Mexico, began to extend their range of influence back toward the north. Some scholars believe that the people called the Mogollon, Hohokam, and Anasazi, who predated the historic southwestern Pueblo Indian cultures, were northern offshoots of the Central Mexican civilizations. The Maya and Aztec are also given credit by some scholars for being the forerunners, or at least heavily influencing, the mound-building Adena and Hopewell cultures of the eastern half of the continental United States.

Texas, lying in the middle of the continent, has felt the influence of cultures from all points of the compass. Its physiography, though dramatically different from its present-day appearance—the pine forests now confined to far East Texas extended then to near Austin; piñon pine groves dotted the Trans-Pecos; and luxuriant grasslands spread across the Central Texas Hill Country, to name three instances—made an inviting picture of plenty for nomadic peoples with an early stone-age technology.

The first Texans dressed themselves in skins or wore simple coverings woven from plant fibers, when they bothered to dress at all. Some of them lived in low, hide-covered tepees, but for most of them home was a lean-to covered with branches or grass mats. When traveling, all of them used such simple shelters.

These people moved about looking for sustenance in prescribed territories carved out by agreement with their neighbors or determined by that time-honored human tradition of taking from those who have what you want. Although their fate was shaped by the whims of the weather more than we could imagine today, only during a drought or following a late freeze were they unable to find anything to eat. They rarely went without food because they ate everything. They took small game in traps, with nets, or with throwing sticks not too different from boomerangs. Larger game was killed with lances, sometimes held and thrusted, sometimes thrown. Thomas R. Hester, in his book *Digging into South Texas Prehistory*, lists foods eaten by one group of early Texans: sixteen seeds and fruits, twelve mammals (the black-tailed jackrabbit being the largest, the rest, except for the gray fox, being small rodents), six species of fish, seventeen different species of snakes and the blue spiny lizard. The lizard was either the most numerous or the easiest to catch, its bones being predominant among the reptiles. Remains of all these foods were found at the Golondrina Complex Hearth, Baker Cave, in Val Verde County.

Although the early Texans were wanderers, their travels were seldom at random. In general the bands moved through familiar countryside, regularly visiting locations that were sources of particular foods. For instance, the pecan groves in the bottomlands of the Colorado River were regular points of call for the Tonkawas. There was, north of the present-day town of Alice, an area where prickly pear cactus grew in such abundance that Indian groups from all around would gather in the late summer to harvest the ripening tunas or cactus fruit.

The hunters in the wandering Texas tribes developed weapons that made them effective killers of the small game which were a substantial part of their diet. In particular, they used a light spear, about three feet long, thrown with the aid of an atlatl, a wondrously simple invention which had the effect of making the thrower's arm two feet longer and adding an extra elbow. With this device, the hunter could add up to twice the leverage to an overhand throw, greatly increasing its speed and power. The effect of the atlatl was similar to that achieved by a jai-alai player, rocketing the ball out of his basket-shaped glove with stunning speed.

The "arrowheads" modern-day Texans are so pleased to find were actually points for the short spears used with the atlatl. Both long and short spears went out of vogue somewhat when the bow and arrow was introduced. The projectile points called "bird arrowheads" today were indeed used with arrows, but they were general purpose arrowheads, used against everything from birds to deer to fish. Along with improvements in the technology of delivering projectiles came refinements in the craft of flint-working. This ancient craft only began to lose its importance when iron was introduced by Europeans.

Before the introduction of the horse, aborigines of the northern plains used a hunting technique called a "jump" or "fall" to kill large numbers of mammoths, camels or bison. Using geological features, or oftentimes building walls of brush or rock up to a mile long, the Indians would construct a funnel-shaped corral with its small end at the edge of a cliff. A herd of animals was lured or driven into position between the two ends of the corral and, at the proper moment, they were stampeded to the small end and over the cliff. Those not killed by the fall were dispatched with lances, the points of which sometimes came off in the animals. For today's scientists, the discovery of those points in the company of animal bones confirms the kill as human. Two geographic features were required for this technique to be practiced: plentiful grasslands supporting large herds and a terrain with a cliff of respectable height.

The only confirmed kills of this kind in Texas took place at the Bonfire Shelter site in Mile Canyon, near present-day Langtry in Val Verde County. Ten thousand or more years ago, this region was rolling grassland, cooler and wetter than it is today, a prime habitat for herds of big herbivores. Evidence indicates that more than ten thousand years ago bison were intentionally driven over this cliff and killed and butchered on this site, not just once, but maybe as many as three times. Then, eight thousand years later, the trap was used again.

The vastness of the time gap was probably the result of a climatic change. Fluctuations in weather patterns may have left the countryside hot and dry, much as it is today. Unable to find enough to eat, the herds of big animals might have moved back to the north. A passage of eight thousand years may have seen the climate cool down, the rains come again, and with them the herds. The Indians, who had stayed and lived on what the country offered, knew a good thing when they saw it and drove a herd right back to the same cliff at Bonfire Shelter.

On the plains, where buffalo were plentiful, and in the Texas Hill Country, where they were occasional visitors, the Tonkawas and Apaches took them where they could find them. Most kills here occurred when the big animals became mired in mud near water holes or when an animal was physically disabled beforehand through no action by the Indians. Not only did the early Texans take advantage of any injured or mired animals they came across; they, like aborigines on all continents, would also chase other predators off a kill and take it for themselves. If there was real hunger in the band, they were not above making a meal of any carrion they came across.

Early Texas Indians sometimes became the prey of wild animals. A country like early Texas, rich in animal protein, was populated with predators happy to take advantage of the bounty. Bears, panthers, wolves, and coyotes were in particular evidence in Texas, along with smaller predators like ocelots and bobcats.

The clothing worn by prehistoric Texans was limited to what was needed to protect the wearer from extremes of weather. As might be expected, among a wandering people, footwear merited special attention. Most tribes did not use moccasins but rather their women fashioned sandals from fibers woven into a thick platform. The sandal had a strap that slipped over the foot above the toe joint and an arrangement that came up on either side of the ankle. Cords were tied in front or behind the ankle, probably depending upon individual preference. Given the speed with which sturdy hide moccasins wore out, the women of early Texas tribes must have had a full-time job keeping everybody in the fragile sandals.

The lot of the aboriginal woman in Texas was much the same as it was elsewhere. Women tended the hearth, bore the children and cared for them, tanned hides and wove cloth-like garments from plant fibers, and packed and unpacked the meager goods that were moved on an almost daily basis. When a band moved, the women did most of the carrying. Dogs, the only animal the Indians ever domesticated besides the horse, were fitted with miniature travois that dragged the ground behind them and were loaded with as much as the animal could pull. Sometimes packs were fitted to the dogs, much like a pack on a burro or mule, but the travois was probably the preferred choice since it carried more.

Births were the province of the women. The mother-to-be, with two or three friends and supporters, would go to a place away from the camp for the event. A routine birth was an occasion for great joy; it was always a pleasure to welcome another member to the band. The mortality rate, however, was ghastly high and the aborigine who made it through birth and out of infancy was a sturdy individual to say the least. The nomadic Indians were practical people and unpleasant things happened at births. If the mother died in delivery and no wet nurse was available, the baby was killed. Deformities that would make the child a burden on the band usually meant death. Some Indians considered twins a bad omen, and they were both doomed. The basis for this may have been the obvious difficulty involved in caring for twins.

Most of the first Texans used grave yards, laying bodies to rest in the same area time and again. At Oso Creek, near Corpus Christi, the remains of over a hundred individuals were unearthed in the 1930s. Some of the bones lay atop earlier burials, indicating long term use of the site. The usual manner of burial was to lay the body on its side, in a fetal position with the hands covering the face. Material goods have almost never been found with the bones, not surprising in a culture of nomads who had little in the way of worldly goods to begin with. Though there is no specific record of such, we can assume that the recently departed were sent off to the spirit world with the assistance of a shaman. The Indians were great believers in the spirit world and it is hard to imagine any occasion like a funeral without some sort of ceremony.

Burials in other parts of Texas differed, probably because of terrain more than religious beliefs. In far western Texas, bodies were buried in caves or wedged into crevices in the sides of cliffs and covered as well as possible with rocks and other debris. On the plains the body was buried in a shallow grave, or it was wrapped and placed on a raised platform, away from predators. In many parts of the state, however, there were specific areas used for burials to keep the spirits in one place. The Indian did not spend more time than was necessary around these places, fearing that the ones gone before would want to take the living with them.

Some tribes believed that all things, animate and inanimate, had spirits of their own. They all believed in a supreme deity; the Karankawa reportedly believed in two. These held sway over all the others. It was the duty of the shaman to act as intermediary between the band and the spirits—or gods—in important matters such as weather, hunting, food, and so on. The individual Indian could talk directly to the spirit on personal matters but the larger concerns needed official magic. If the appeal by the shaman was not answered in the hoped for matter, it was assumed that the shaman didn't ask properly, not that the group was deemed unworthy of positive consideration. So the process was refined and repeated and sure enough, sooner or later it would start or stop raining.

Indian life in Texas during the centuries leading up to the European intrusion followed two distinctly different courses. In the east the Caddos enjoyed the benefit of regular harvests. An industrious, well-organized society living in fixed villages year after year, they were what we would term "well off." At the western end of the state, the Jumanos enjoyed the benefits of a similar agricultural base, together with long-established traditions passed on from their cousins to the west. In the vast land between the two agricultural peoples, lived the nomads. Hunters and gatherers by choice or by the dictates of the environment, their way of life remained largely unchanged for centuries.

Let's examine these tribes—their customs and conditions—before the white man's arrival.

The Jumano of the Trans-Pecos lived and farmed in the canyons of the Rio Grande and were the easternmost extension of the Mogollon Pueblo culture. They were the first Texas tribe to feel the weight of Spanish influence on the New World, excepting the few who came into contact with Cabeza de Vaca along the Gulf Coast. The Trans-Pecos (that area of Texas west of the Pecos River) was not the arid desert land that we know today. In the time of the Jumano it was an hospitable land where they dry-farmed maize, beans, squash, and tobacco with success. These people lived in adobe and rock structures.

The Lipan Apache and their close kin the Jicarilla and Mescalero Apache made up the eastern branch of this famous tribe. Identifying their exact range in prehistory has stumped scholars for years. Each Spanish expedition that entered their supposed range came back with a list of names for the Indians they found, most of them appearing for the first time. Suffice it to say that the Lipan lived in western Texas and eastern New Mexico, ranging the Llano Estacado and the western plains almost to the Santa Fe-Taos region and sometimes as far east as the Balcones Fault in western Central Texas.

The Caddo of East Texas were the most advanced of the Texas aborigines. They lived in established villages where they grew and harvested maize, beans, pumpkins, tobacco, and a variety of other vegetables. Their culture resembled that of tribes of advanced mound builders in the southeastern United States. Close parallels can be drawn between the Caddos and the Natchez Indians of Mississippi. Their language was one that was similar to, if not the same as, languages used as far north as Kansas and as far to the east as the Atlantic coast. Some anthropologists have suggested that the Caddo culture made its entrance into the present United States via a water route along the western Gulf coast, which leads to speculation about Olmec-Maya origins. Whether the Caddo—and the whole Southeastern Cultural Complex—are the product of a splinter group from Central Mexico or the result of coincidental evolution is unprovable at this time. Where they came from is of little consequence to this discussion. The point is that they were there when the Europeans arrived and although in decline, were clearly the most sophisticated of the peoples in Texas. The Texas Caddos were only one of two major centers of the Caddo culture, the other being in present-day Arkansas.

The Karankawa's territory was along the coast of Texas, roughly 75 to 100 miles north and south of Matagorda Bay. They were a hunter-gatherer tribe, roving in small bands through the estuaries and coastal plains and on occasion venturing out to the barrier islands. In groups of up to thirty or forty individuals, they followed the ripening flora in this area, subsisting largely on what plant life was available and the shell fish and fish they could find or catch. Sporadic forays inland allowed them to enjoy antelope or rabbit or the rare buffalo, but they were in the main, a marine-oriented people. They made dugout canoes and wove mats from grasses for covering lean-to shelters and spreading as sleeping pads. They were much maligned by their neighbors, principally because of their practice of using the grease of alligators to ward off mosquitos. The rancid smell, apparently, was offensive to everybody but another Karankawa. They were accused of cannibalism, though they were shocked and revolted to find that some of the castaways with Cabeza de Vaca had eaten the flesh of dead companions. There is no doubt that they did practice ritual cannibalism but among the Indians of Texas and aborigines the world over they were hardly alone. There are written accounts from the late nineteenth century of Tonkawas, acting as scouts for Texas Rangers in pursuit of Comanche raiders, ritually eating portions of their victims, and inviting the Rangers to join in. The accounts say the Rangers declined. Perhaps because of their repugnant smell and probably because of their ferociousness in battle, the Karankawa were hated by most of their neighbors. Adding the smell and their fierce reputation to the charges of cannibalism made them seem something less than human. As W. W. Newcomb points out in *The Indians of Texas*, it becomes easier for one group of people to despise another if the latter can be considered sub-human.

The Tonkawa of Central Texas appear to have been the descendants of the original human settlers of the area. They were also the southernmost peoples of the Great Plains buffalo culture. They were red meat eaters, buffalo being their diet staple along with deer and everything else they could kill save wolves and coyotes, which escaped the cooking fire only because of a religious taboo. They used available plants as their foraging neighbors did and fish as the Karankawa did. Never very numerous, the Tonkawa seem to have lived in relative peace with the people around them. It is known that they often traded with the Caddos and a band of the Tonkawa is recorded to have joined a segment of the Karankawas, intermarrying and becoming, for all practical purposes, Karankawa. They lived in short, rude, hide tepees in the winter and conical brush shelters in the summer. Apparently they fell under the spell of their habitat in the Texas Hill Country, for it seems that they enjoyed the casual lifestyle that is still prevalent in that part of the world. Their language remains a mystery, having no discoverable linguistic relationship to any other in the whole of the Americas. Some scholars have suggested that it was akin to the speech of the Coahuiltecans, but since the Coahuiltecan language died off without record, there is no way of proving this thesis. This is unusual, since other Indian dialects show recognizable inter-relationships.

The Coahuiltecans were never a tribe in the traditional sense, but rather a collection of small scattered bands who happened to speak a related language called Coahuilteco. These constantly wandering hunters and gatherers lived in

South Texas, an area defined by drawing a line across the state from the mouth of the Trinity River east of Houston to the point where the Pecos River empties into the Rio Grande. The area south of this line as far as the Rio Grande was Coahuiltecan Texas. It represents only the northern reach of this remarkable group of people who made a living from a land that was at times as unforgiving as any on the planet. The remainder of their area covered the modern Mexican states of Tamaulipas, Nuevo Leon, the northeastern parts of Coahuila and Zacatecas and northern San Luis Potosi. These people, who were part of the Western Gulf Culture, developed precious little in the way of technology. They wandered over the land, living from meal to meal, in a part of the world where the bountiful earth is cleverly camouflaged. Through trial and error, they learned when and where plant life was ready to be eaten. They discovered or invented ways and means to capture and kill a variety of small mammals and reptiles, and they had no aversion to fish. For that matter, they had little aversion to anything. They made the most of a habitat that offered the least. They knew, for example, that the native pecan trees put forth a bumper crop every three years, so they learned how to cache the leftovers for the lean times. On the other hand they never tried to improve on a solution or an invention once they found one that worked. What technology they had never grew past the most basic level. There have been found, in houses built by the Spanish and occupied by Coahuiltecans, stone projectile points made in the manner of a far older people. Though Cabeza de Vaca marveled at their adaptability to the heat and cold and at their remarkable stamina, this whole race was unable to survive the leap from the stone age to the nineteenth century. The last of these ancient people died over a hundred years ago.

INDIANS IN TEXAS 1500

THIS PLACE WILL ONE DAY BE CALLED SOUTH TEXAS, AND THE DESCEN-
DANTS OF THESE PEOPLE WILL BE CALLED INDIANS, BUT NOW, IN
THE TIME OF THE **AGARITA** BERRY'S RIPENING, THEY ARE AN
EXTENDED FAMILY GROUP OF COAHUILTECO SPEAKING ABORI-
GINES, ENJOYING THE WARMTH OF THE EARLY SUMMER SUN
AFTER A COLD AND WET WINTER IN

PRE·HISTORY

LIKE THEIR FATHERS BEFORE THEM, THEY SPEND THEIR LIVES WANDER-
ING FROM PLACE TO PLACE, FOLLOWING THE SEASONS, MARKING THE
TIME OF YEAR BY THE RIPENING OF THE CHOICEST EDIBLE PLANTS.
BECAUSE THEY ARE NOMADS AND AFOOT, THEY CAN CARRY BUT
LITTLE IN THE WAY OF SUSTENANCE AND MUST TRULY LIVE OFF THE
LAND. BUT FOR THE ACORNS, WALNUTS, PECANS AND MESQUITE
BEANS CACHED ABOUT THEIR TERRITORY, TIMES OF LITTLE RAIN
WOULD MEAN GREAT SUFFERING.
  THEY ARE MOVING SOUTH NOW TO A FAVORED RIVER SITE,
WHERE THE ACORNS WILL BE COMING TO A USEABLE AGE AND THE
SQUIRRELS AND RACCOONS ARE PLENTIFUL AND THEY CAN ENJOY, FOR
A TIME, A LIFE OF LEISURE AND PLENTY.

  THEY ARE ALSO ON A MISSION. ONE IMPORTANT TO EVERY MEM-
BER OF THE BAND. A MISSION THEY BEGAN THE PAST FALL AND WILL
NOW, FINALLY, BE ABLE TO COMPLETE.

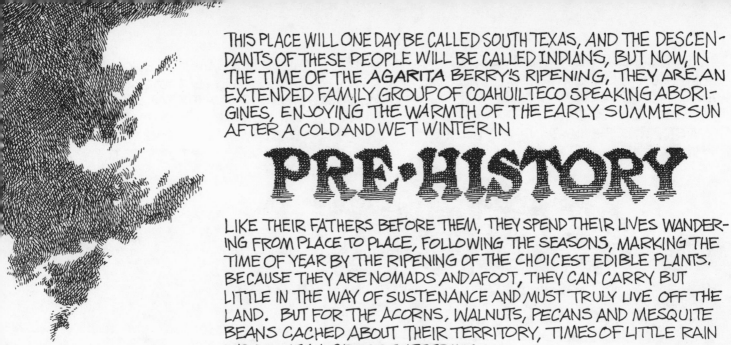

17

IN MID-AFTERNOON THEY COME UPON SOME SPRINGS BUBBLING FROM THE WALL OF A SINK HOLE. THE CRYSTAL CLEAR POOL AND INVITING SHADE OF THE LIMESTONE OVERHANG BID THEM STOP FOR THE NIGHT AND THEY ACCEPT THE INVITATION.

WHILE THE YOUNGSTERS GATHER FIREWOOD, THE WOMEN MAKE CAMP. THEY PLAN TO ROAST THE REMAINING HAUNCH OF A WHITE TAIL DEER KILLED THE DAY BEFORE. MEANWHILE, THEY BUSY THEMSELVES WITH SPREADING THE SLEEPING MATS, WOVEN FROM FIBERS STRIPPED FROM THE SOTOL PLANT.

TWO WARRIORS TAKE THE OPPORTUNITY TO CLIMB A NEARBY HILL AND SCOUR IT FOR FLINT. THEY WILL MAKE REPLACEMENT ARROW HEADS AND TOOLS BY THE LIGHT OF THE FIRE SHOULD THEIR HUNT PROVE FRUITFUL.

THE GRANDFATHER SITS APART WITH A TIGHTLY BOUND BUNDLE HE HAS CARRIED WITH HIM FOR THE LAST FOUR MONTHS. HE STARES STRAIGHT AHEAD, OBLIVIOUS TO THE ACTIVITY AROUND HIM.

THE ABORIGINES DO NOT SIT DOWN AROUND THE CAMPFIRE AND EAT TOGETHER. THEY EAT AS THEY ARE MOVED TO, COMING AND GOING FROM SELF-APPOINTED TASKS: THE WOMEN CARING FOR THE CHILDREN, REFILLING THE BUFFALO STOMACH CANTEENS WITH WATER FOR TOMORROW; THE MEN INVESTIGATING REAL AND IMAGINED SOUNDS IN THE DEEPENING NIGHT.

FINALLY, ALL ARE FED AND IT IS TIME FOR THE STORIES TO BEGIN — OF HUNTS AND FIGHTS AND WATER WITCHES AND VISIONS AND OF THE OLD ONES AND THE OLD WAYS. IN THIS WAY, AN ORAL TRADITION KEEPS A CULTURE ALIVE.

ALL THE WHILE, THE GRANDFATHER KEEPS HIS OWN COUNCIL, EATING ONLY WHAT IS BROUGHT HIM — STAYING CLOSE BY HIS PRECIOUS BUNDLE.

SUNRISE SEES THE CAMP ASTIR, AND THE CLOUDLESS BLUE SKY FORECASTS A FINE DAY FOR TRAVEL.

THEY FIT THE SMALL TRAVOIS TO THE CAMP DOGS, MAKING THE BURDEN LIGHTER FOR THE WOMEN. THE MEN LEAD THE WAY, WITH SOME IN THE REAR AND OTHERS ON THE FLANKS AS GUARDS. THEY HAVE HUMAN ENEMIES, BUT THE MAIN FUNCTION OF THE GUARD IS TO WATCH FOR PREDATORY ANIMALS. IN A COUNTRY WHERE DEER, ANTELOPE AND BUFFALO ABOUND, BEAR AND PANTHERS DO TOO. BEAR AND PANTHERS THOUGH, TAKE THEIR MEALS WHERE THEY FIND THEM, AND THEY FIND AN INDIAN JUST AS TASTY AS AN ANTELOPE AND NOT NEARLY AS HARD TO CATCH.

SOME OF THE MEN WANDER AFIELD OF THE MARCH, AND BY THE TIME THEY CAMP FOR THE NIGHT, THESE HUNTERS WILL HAVE TAKEN AN EVEN DOZEN COTTON TAIL RABBITS FOR THE FIRE.

ALONG THE MARCH, THE WOMEN KEEP WATCH FOR ROOTS AND RIPENING BERRIES, PARTICULARLY THE FAVORED MUSTANG GRAPE, WHOSE SWEET MEAT MAKES GETTING PAST THE BITTER SKIN WORTH THE EFFORT. THE PERSIMMONS ARE STILL GREEN AND HARD, BUT BEFORE LONG, THEY WILL BE ADDED TO THE DIET.

THE GRANDFATHER WALKS ALONE.

IN THE NEXT DAYS THEY CROSS THE DRAINAGE OF A CYPRESS-LINED RIVER AND MOVING AT AN EASY PACE, THEY ARE BROUGHT UP SHORT BY THE SIGHT THEY SEE FROM THE TOP OF A RISE.

BELOW THEM IS A BUFFALO BULL. SERIOUSLY INJURED, PROBABLY IN A FIGHT OVER A HAREM OR PERHAPS A FALL FROM THIS SAME STEEP HILL, THE ANIMAL IS ON HIS BELLY, BREATHING HEAVILY. HIS HINDQUARTERS ARE IMMOBILE FROM A BROKEN BACK.

LEAVING THEIR PACKS ON THE RISE, THE HUNTERS MOVE QUICKLY TO TAKE ADVANTAGE OF THIS WINDFALL, BUT THEY MOVE WITH CAUTION TOO, FOR AS BADLY HURT AS HE IS, A BUFFALO BULL IS NOTHING TO TRIFLE WITH.

IN SHORT ORDER THE BULL IS DISPATCHED AND, JOINED BY THE REMAINDER OF THE
BAND, THE HUNTERS CLAIM THE PRIZE OF THE WARM RAW LIVER DIPPED IN THE
SWEET BILE OF THE STOMACH.

THE WOMEN BEGIN TO DRESS THE CARCASS AND THE BAND MAKES CAMP EARLY,
FOR THIS IS AN OCCASION FOR CELEBRATION. ROASTED BUFFALO HUMP RIBS AND
BOILED TONGUE WILL BE ENJOYED BY ALL TO THE POINT OF BURSTING.

ALL SAVE THE GRANDFATHER, WHO SITS DOWN BESIDE AN OAK TREE, GENTLY
LAYING HIS BUNDLE CLOSE BY HIS SIDE.

A BUFFALO IS A MIGHTY AMOUNT OF CREATURE, EVEN FOR A WANDERING, HUNGRY BAND OF ABORIGINES. SO THE GROUP LAYS OVER FOR A FEW DAYS, DOING FULL JUSTICE TO THE CARCASS. WHILE IN THE NEIGHBORHOOD, THEY EMPTY A NEARBY CACHE OF LAST YEAR'S PECANS AND THE WOMEN AND CHILDREN SPEND BALMY AFTERNOONS SHELLING THE NUTS AND STRINGING THE HALVES FOR FUTURE USE. AND ON A BOULDER NOT FAR AWAY, THE MEN CARVE A RECORD OF THE EVENT AND A TRIBUTE TO THE GREAT, GIVING SPIRIT OF THE BUFFALO.

LIKE ALL ABORIGINES, THESE MAKE THE MOST OF A BIG ANIMAL KILL. BESIDES THE FOOD FROM THE MEAT AND ORGANS, THEY TAN THE HIDE FOR WINTER ROBES. THEY STRIP THE SINEW FROM THE BONES FOR BOWSTRINGS AND CORDS. THE BONES ARE CRACKED OPEN, EXPOSING THE RICH MARROW WHICH IS EAGERLY EATEN. THE DOGS SLIP IN AND OUT FOR WHAT MORSELS THEY CAN GET.

THEY FASHION DIGGING TOOLS FROM THE FLAT SCAPULA AND PELVIC BONES, AND A LITTLE WORK ON ONE END TURNS A RIB INTO A SCRAPER OR BACK SCRATCHER. THE HORNS BECOME CONTAINERS.

FAT IS RENDERED, THEN MIXED WITH PECAN PIECES AND MEAT SCRAPS, SHAPED INTO BALLS A LITTLE LARGER THAN GOLF BALLS, AND STORED FOR USE LATER.

ON THE THIRD DAY COMPANY COMES! ANOTHER WANDERING BAND OF COAHUILTECANS IS ESCORTED INTO THE CAMPSITE.

ONE OF THE NEW ARRIVALS IS A SISTER, AND TWO OTHERS ARE COUSINS, SO THE COMBINED GROUP TAKES ON ALL THE ASPECTS OF A FAMILY REUNION. IN THIS MATRIARCHAL SO-CIETY, THE HUSBAND LIVES WITH THE WIFE'S FAMILY, AND THOUGH HE AND HIS FAMILY MAY TRAVEL SEPARATELY AT TIMES, HE IS OBLI-GATED TO HER PARENTS. THIS INSURES THAT THE OLD PEOPLE WILL HAVE A PROVIDER.

AT THE FIRESIDE THAT NIGHT, THE NEWCOMERS TELL STRANGE TALES OF TWO WHITE GODS WITH WHITE EYES AND ONE BLACK GOD — BLACK ALL OVER — WHO CAME OUT OF THE GREAT SALTY WATER WHERE THE SUN IS BORN. THESE GODS HAD MIGHTY MAGIC AND HEALED THE SICK AND WOUNDED AS THEY WANDERED AMONG THE TRIBES.

THOUGH EVERYONE KNOWS THAT ALL THINGS HAVE THEIR OWN SPIRIT, THIS TALE IS VERY HARD TO BELIEVE, AND WHILE THE STORY IS TOLD IN ALL SERIOUSNESS, AND IS LISTENED TO POLITELY, WHEN ALL GO TO SLEEP THAT NIGHT, THE BUFFALO KILLERS ARE SMILING TO THEM- SELVES AT THE GREAT JOKE THAT HAS BEEN PLAYED ON THEM.

THE GRANDFATHER, AT HIS PLACE UNDER THE OAK AND BY HIS BUNDLE, HAS PAID NO HEED TO ANY OF IT.

AT MID-MORNING THE TWO BANDS ARE PACKED AND READY TO GO THEIR SEPARATE WAYS. ONE FAMILY FROM THE NEW GROUP WILL JOIN THE BUFFALO KILLERS. THE WIFE IS NEARING TIME TO GIVE BIRTH TO HER FIRST CHILD AND AT FIFTEEN YEARS OF AGE, SHE SEEKS THE COMPANY OF HER OLDER SISTER, THE SECOND WIFE OF ONE OF THE FIRST BAND'S HUNTERS. THE OLD FAMILIAR FACE WILL MAKE THE ORDEAL OF BIRTH IF NOT MORE COMFORTABLE, AT LEAST LESS TERRIFYING.

TAKING THEIR PLACE IN THE LINE OF MARCH, THE WOMEN VISIT AND KEEP A CLOSE WATCH ON THE CHILDREN.

FOR THEIR PART, THE MEN OF THE BAND ARE ALWAYS HAPPY TO WELCOME A NEW HUNTER WITH HIS NEW STORIES.

BY LATE AFTERNOON
THEY HAVE REACHED THEIR
DESTINATION.
HERE THE GRAND-
FATHER STOPS AND LAYS
HIS BURDEN DOWN.
WITHIN SIGHT IS
THE ANCIENT BURIAL
GROUND WHERE THE
BONES OF ALL THE OLD
ONES LIE.
HE HAS BROUGHT
THE BUNDLE HOME, HE
HAS KEPT THE FAITH.

WHILE THE WOMEN MAKE CAMP
BESIDE THE RIVER, THE GRAND-
FATHER RETRIEVES A SMALL
BUCKSKIN SACK FROM A PAR-
FLECHE AMONG THE BAGGAGE.
SITTING DOWN FACING HIS BUN-
DLE, HE REACHES INTO THE
SACK AND WITHDRAWS FIVE
SMALLER SACKS.

ON A FLAT ROCK PICKED
ESPECIALLY FOR THIS PURPOSE
HE MEASURES OUT FIVE PILES
OF GREASE FROM THE NEWLY
KILLED BUFFALO.

GOING TO EACH SACK IN
TURN, HE SPRINKLES THE
BLACK POWDER OF CHARCOAL
ON ONE PILE; THE FINE, RED-
ORANGE DUST SCRAPED FROM
UNDER LIMESTONE OVERHANGS
ON ANOTHER.

THE GROUND RESIDUE OF
DRIED BLUE BERRIES, THE
FINELY POWDERED, ELECTRIC
YELLOW FROM THE HEART OF
THE AGARITA BUSH AND THE
FINE, PURE DUST OF WHITE
LIMESTONE GO ON THE LAST
GREASE PILES.

AS HE BLENDS THE
COLOR INTO THE GREASE,
BINDING THE TWO TOGETHER,
HE BEGINS TO CHANT.

HIS CONCENTRATION IS SUCH THAT HE FAILS TO NOTICE THE FOUR WOMEN WHO PASS WITHIN A FEW FEET OF HIM, EVEN THOUGH THE ONE HEAVY WITH CHILD IS BENT HALF OVER, GASPING AND SOBBING IN PAIN.

THE GRANDFATHER IS JOINED BY TWO BOYS WHO WILL HELP HIM WITH THE CERE-MONY. THE APPRENTICE SHAMANS BUILD A SMALL FIRE, THEN TAKE THEIR PLACES FACING THE OLD MAN.

HE DIPS TWO FINGERS INTO THE BLACK MIXTURE AND BEGINS TO OUT-LINE THE MYSTICAL DESIGNS ON HIS FACE AND BODY.

WHILE A HUNDRED YARDS
AWAY, IN THICK BRUSH,
ANOTHER ORDEAL
BEGINS IN EARNEST...

THE OLD MAN CONTINUES TO PAINT HIMSELF THROUGH THE NIGHT, AND WHEN THE FIRE IS ALL BUT GONE, IN THE COOL GREY LIGHT OF A DEWY DAWN, HE APPLIES THE FINAL STROKE AND HIS CHANT COMES TO AN END.

IN THE THICKET, THE STRUGGLE OF A NEW LIFE TO BEGIN HAS LEFT THE FIFTEEN YEAR OLD MOTHER-TO-BE ON THE EDGE OF EXHAUSTION. HER SISTER STROKES HER HAIR AND OFFERS SOOTHING WORDS BUT THE LABOR IS LONG AND NO PROGRESS IS APPARENT.

THE WOMEN HAVE COME AND GONE ALL NIGHT LONG, OFFERING UP THEIR ADVICE FROM EXPERIENCE AND SUCH POTIONS AS THEY COULD CALL TO MIND.

AS THE SUN COMES UP, THE SITUATION IN THE BRUSH IS CRITICAL. THE BABY IS TOO LARGE AND IDEAS ARE NO LONGER COMING.

FROM A SECOND PARFLECHE IN THE OLD MAN'S
BAGGAGE THE BOYS TAKE A NECKLACE MADE
OF ALTERNATING CLAWS OF GRIZZLY BEAR
AND MOUNTAIN LION. THEN ANOTHER NECK-
LACE MADE OF HUMAN FINGER BONES, BORED
HOLLOW AND ETCHED WITH GEOMETRIC
DESIGNS. NEXT COMES A BELT MADE FROM
THE SKIN OF A DIAMOND BACK RATTLESNAKE
AND TWO RATTLES; ONE MADE FROM A
TURTLE SHELL, THE OTHER FROM A GOURD.
BOTH ARE DECORATED WITH HAIR FROM
THE TAIL OF A BULL BUFFALO AND PAINTED
WITH SNAKE-LIKE DESIGNS.
        THE LAST ITEM IS THE CAPE OF A
DESERT BIG HORN RAM, THE HUGE CURLED
HORNS INTACT. THIS LAST THEY FIT ON THE
GRANDFATHER, TYING IT SNUGLY IN PLACE BY
A THONG REACHING UNDER HIS CHIN.
        EACH BOY TAKES A RATTLE IN HAND,
THE OLD MAN BENDS AND CAREFULLY,
PICKS UP THE BUNDLE, AND THE THREE
WALK TOWARD THE SUN, NOW ABOVE THE
EASTERN HILLS, TO A LOW MOUND JUST IN
FRONT OF THE TREE LINE AT THE BASE OF
THE RISING GROUND.

IN THE BRUSH, THE STRUGGLE IS ENDED. THE TEENAGER LAYS AS IF ASLEEP, HER STRAIGHT DARK HAIR MATTED AGAINST HER WET SKIN. HER SISTER ROCKS TO AND FRO, STARING AHEAD BUT SEEING NOTHING. THE GROUND IS BARE OF LEAVES AND GRASS AND YOU WOULD TAKE THIS SCENE FOR PEACEFUL WERE IT NOT FOR THE DARK, DAMP PUDDLE THAT CONTINUES TO WIDEN BENEATH THE HIPS OF THE PRONE GIRL.

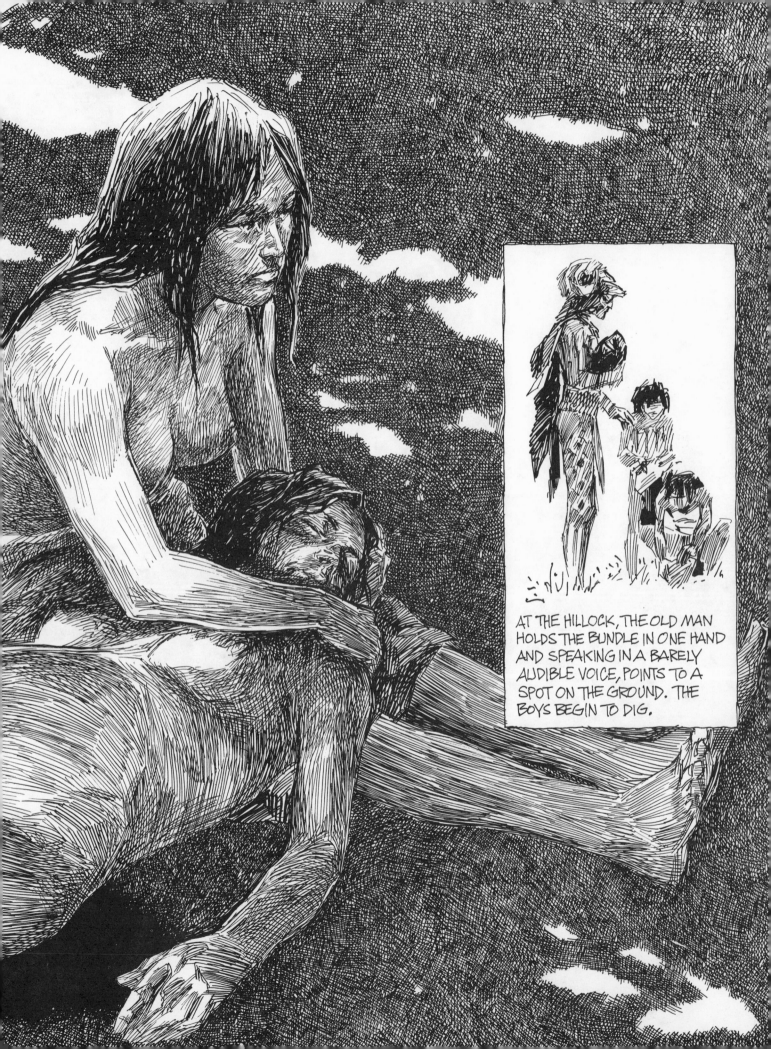

AT THE HILLOCK, THE OLD MAN HOLDS THE BUNDLE IN ONE HAND AND SPEAKING IN A BARELY AUDIBLE VOICE, POINTS TO A SPOT ON THE GROUND. THE BOYS BEGIN TO DIG.

THE NOISE INTERRUPTS THE OLD MAN AND THE BOYS AND ONE OF THE YOUNGSTERS IS SENT TO FIND THE CAUSE, THOUGH THE GRANDFATHER ALREADY KNOWS. HE HAS FELT THIS COMING.

A CONFERENCE IS HELD AMONG THE MEN, AND WHEN TWO OF THE WOMEN ARE CALMED ENOUGH, THEY GO TO THE THICKET AND PREPARE THE GIRL'S BODY FOR BURIAL.

ON THE HILLOCK NOW, THE BAND GATHERS AROUND THE RECTANGULAR HOLE SCRAPED IN THE SHALLOW DIRT BY THE TWO BOYS. THE DEAD GIRL IS LAID IN THE BOTTOM, A STRING OF SHELL BEADS AROUND HER NECK, THE DIRT AND GRIME WASHED FROM HER BODY BY THE WOMEN; HER FACE PAINTED RED. ON HER CHEST IS A HANDFUL OF FLOWERS, GATHERED AND PLACED THERE BY HER STILL GRIEVING SISTER.

THE OLD MAN SETS THE BUNDLE AT HER FEET, AND UNTYING IT, LAYS THE WRAPPING BACK AND EXPOSES THE SKULL AND BONES OF HIS PREDECESSOR, THE SHAMAN-TEACHER WHO DIED SO FAR FROM THIS SACRED PLACE.

HOLDING THE SKULL HIGH OVERHEAD SO THE SPIRIT CAN SEE HE IS HOME, THE GRANDFATHER BEGINS A CHANT THAT IS TAKEN UP BY THE REST OF THE BAND.

THE BONES AND SKULL ARE PLACED IN THE GRAVE ON THE GIRL'S LAP AND ALL IS COVERED.

THEY'LL LAY HERE WITH THE BONES OF OTHERS OF THEIR KIND, THEIR HEADS POINTED EAST, THEIR FEET WEST, IN THE OLD WAY.

THE BAND PACKS TO LEAVE IMMEDIATELY. THEY HAVE SURELY DISTURBED SOME OLD GHOSTS AND TO LINGER HERE WOULD BE TO COURT BAD LUCK FOR ALL. BY NIGHTFALL THEY ARE FAR SOUTH, OUT OF THE RIVER VALLEY AND MOVING TO THE WEST. THE COLD CAMP THEY MAKE THAT NIGHT IS WITHOUT PLEASURE. THEY ARE QUIET, THE CHILDREN FAST ASLEEP FROM THE RIGORS OF THE DAY—EVEN THE DOGS SENSE THE SOMBER MOOD.

BY MORNING THE CAMP HAS TAKEN ON A NEW SPIRIT. THE CHILDREN ARE UP AND HUNGRY— SO HUNGRY THEY SETTLE FOR COLD RATIONS WITH BARELY A GRUMBLE.

BEFORE THE LINE OF MARCH IS SET UP, THE HUNTERS ARE LONG SINCE OUT. THERE ARE MOUTHS TO FEED AND PLACES TO GO AND LONG MOURNINGS ARE A LUXURY FOR ANOTHER TIME.

FOUR SUMMERS LATER, WHILE
CROSSING A LOOSE, SANDY
PLAIN, THE ABORIGINES
WILL SEE SOMETHING THEY
CANNOT UNDERSTAND.

THIS BAND—ALL OF
WHOM KNOW EVERY TWIST
AND TURN OF EVERY ROCK
AND WHAT CAUSES EVERY
IMPRINT ON THE EARTH—
IS AT A LOSS.

NONE OF THEM CAN
IDENTIFY THE TRACK THEY
HAVE COME ACROSS. THEY
DON'T EVEN AGREE ON WHAT
DIRECTION THE MAKER IS
TAKING.

THEY DEBATE THIS
MARK AT LENGTH, SCANNING
THE HORIZON, SEARCHING
FOR SOME CLUE AS TO
WHETHER THIS SPIRIT IS
GOOD OR EVIL, THE ONE
THAT MADE THE PRINT OF
THE SHOD HORSE.

BOOK TWO . . . 1600–1836

In 1511 Pope Pius II decreed that the native Indians of the New World were, indeed, human beings.

"The Camanchees (sic) are in stature, rather low, and in person, often approaching to corpulency. In their movements, they are heavy and ungraceful; and on their feet, one of the most unattractive and slovenly-looking races of Indians that I have ever seen; but the moment they mount their horses, they seem at once metamorphosed, and surprise the spectator with the ease and elegance of their movements. A Camanchee on his feet is out of his element, and comparatively almost as awkward as a monkey on the ground, without a limb or a branch to cling to; but the moment he lays his hand upon his horse, his <u>face</u>, even, becomes handsome, and he gracefully flies away like a different being."

George Catlin *(1832–1839)*

The horse changed the lives of the aboriginal peoples in Texas forever. Tribes that once dug and scraped for roots in the ground and relied on migrations of large animals became far-ranging hunters of big game. The acquisition of the horse changed social structures within bands as well as relationships between different bands and tribes.

The spread of the horse to the American Indian began in the early part of the seventeenth century when Spanish colonists forced Pueblo Indians to become herdsmen. As livestock will do, some animals strayed and were captured by the Lipan Apaches. Others were helped to stray after the Lipans discovered the advantages of being on horseback on the Llano Estacado, the High Plains of the Texas Panhandle. The Apaches, most likely then, were the first to become fully mounted horse Indians, about 1630 or 1640. By 1690 horses had spread as far as the Texas Gulf Coast and up into the middle of the Great Plains. By 1750 the Crow and Cree in Canada were on horseback and, by 1775, horses had spread to all but the most remote and inhospitable areas west of the Mississippi.

Although the Apaches took readily to the horse, they never raised animals for their own use and for trade. They preferred to let the Spaniards take care of that chore. With ready access to a supply of mounts at Santa Fe and other outposts, they could and did take whatever they wanted. Thus the Spaniards became unwilling suppliers for the Lipan and their cousins the Mescalero and Jicarillo. For nearly a hundred years the Apaches on horseback ruled the territory that was to become Texas, New Mexico, Arizona and northern Mexico. Of the neighboring tribes, the Tonkawas were the only ones who could match the Apache militarily, but they were so heavily outnumbered that their chief tactic was to stay out of the Apaches' path. The Jumanos, subjugated first by the Spaniards, relied upon their masters for protection from the Apaches. The Coahuiltecans, ever reluctant to take up anything new, retreated to the relative safety of the missions being built across the state from El Paso del Norte to near present-day Natchitoches, Louisiana. For their part, the Caddos and Karankawas remained largely out of harm's way by virtue of geography.

Shortly after 1700, however, a new group began to move down from the north to challenge Apache supremacy. The newcomers were known as the Comanches. They acquired horses from the Spaniards and took them onto the Great Plains where they prospered and proliferated. They did almost everything from the back of a horse and at one time every man, woman, and child in the tribe owned as many as six horses, totaling more than a hundred thousand animals. (In contrast, the Southern Cheyenne, known for their breeding and raising successes, rarely approached three animals per person in their herds.)

The Comanches were an offshoot of the Shoshoni, or Snake, tribe of the middle Rocky Mountains. They came into Texas slowly at first, following the buffalo across the Southern Plains, spreading through Kansas and Oklahoma with their great herds of horses. By the time they got to Texas in force they were masters of the horse culture, probably the best the world has ever seen, and they took charge.

The Apache was displaced almost immediately. The Mescalero and Jicarilla bands retreated to the west, leaving the Lipans alone to face the Comanche onslaught. The Lipans pulled back into the Hill Country and the Trans-Pecos, but continued sporadic raids against the Spaniards and fought a holding action against the Comanches into the early 1800s. The incessant warfare took its toll, and when the Anglo-Americans began to move into the state the Lipan Apache was looking for a friend.

Two Lipan statesmen of note emerged from the end of the Apache era. The first was Castro; the second was his son Flacco. Both acted as scouts for, and confidants to, Sam Houston. Both dealt with Noah Smithwick, an early Texas pioneer and faithful recorder of the times, and tried, almost desperately, to save their people from what they correctly saw as impending disaster. Neither lived to see the remnants of the once proud band banished to a reservation in New Mexico.

While the Apaches declined, the Comanches flourished. The old Apache range was perfect for a people who lived on horseback. The canyons and arroyos of West Texas, and most especially Palo Duro Canyon, offered natural corrals. The plains above the canyon served up limitless grass and abounded with game easily run down from the back of a fast pony.

It was from these headquarters that the Comanches made their presence felt. Intrepid travelers, they ranged as far south as the jungles of Central America. Some bands were reported far to the west in the Apache country of Arizona, while their raids to the east carried them to the Texas Gulf Coast. Their northern range stopped along the Arkansas River, whether because of resistance from other tribes or because they were happy with what they had is of little concern. By 1750 the Comanches controlled western Texas and they would continue to dominate it for the next hundred years.

The coming of the Europeans and their horses affected the ages-old distribution of the peoples of Texas in many ways besides allowing the mounted Comanches to move into the region. In 1747 the Wichita, under pressure from the Osage to their north, agreed to a treaty with the Comanches. Engineered by the French, the new alliance established a trading center on the Red River at present-day Spanish Fort. This trading post was fully operational by 1757.

The Wichita, kinsmen to the Pawnee, were made up of several groups: Waco, Tawakoni, Wichita proper and some minor bands whose common denominator was their language, a dialect of Caddoan stock. Living in settled villages, they were mainly farmers, but they were also good horsemen, although never mistaken for Comanches. The French called them "Pani Pique" (tattooed Pawnee) and "Pani Noir" (black Pawnee) because of their dark skin coloration. By 1772 they had settled on the Brazos near Waco and on the Trinity above Palestine. The latter village was abandoned five years later, its inhabitants joining their relatives on the Brazos.

In 1829, raiding Wichitas became so troublesome to Stephen F. Austin's colony that Austin felt moved to make a pact with the local Cherokee, Shawnee and Delaware for the express purpose of ridding the region of Wichita raiders. Their plan was never carried out due to the opposition of the Mexican authorities, though Austin's agreement with the Indians stood.

In East Texas's piney woods, Europeans who met the Caddos for the first time ran into a buzz saw. Encounters in 1541 with De Soto and in 1542 with Moscoso, De Soto's successor, ended in pitched battles. Both parties agreed to disagree and leave one another alone—for the time being. When the Europeans arrived, the agricultural Caddos, despite their sophisticated social order of priests and rulers and workers, were but a pale reflection of their former glory. They had stopped building the flat topped earthen temple mounds but continued their customs of communal planting and harvesting, as well as saving seed and storing grains and produce for winter months. Though they relied mainly on a vegetable diet, they also made use of the abundant fish and game that surrounded them.

They used and apparently invented the same trotline fishing rig that is used in East Texas and throughout the Southeast today. They were expert deer hunters and took black bears for grease and hides, but curiously, did not eat the meat. When they acquired the horse, the Caddos found buffalo easier to hunt and the long distances to the herds in Central Texas became less difficult to traverse.

A strong culture on the wane when first contact with the Spaniards was made, the Caddos were barely noted by the Anglos three hundred years later. Like most Indian groups, this intelligent and energetic people fell prey to European disease. Their great misfortune was that they lived in a part of the country which was contended ground—first between France and Spain, then France and Mexico, and finally the United States and Mexico.

Never numerous like the Comanches or powerful like the Caddos, the little known Atakapans lived on the Coastal Plain and along the Gulf Coast from Galveston Bay to Sabine Pass. Situated as they were between the Caddo to the north and the Karankawa to the south, this group is difficult to identify and its cultural identity is equally hard to define. Simars de Bellisle, a young Frenchman who survived shipwreck and near starvation only to be captured by the Atakapans, wrote of his adventures after the Caddos aided him in his subsequent escape. Much of what we know comes from his remarkable tale.

The word "Atakapan" means "man-eaters" in the Choctaw language, and these Indians probably originated in what is now the southeastern United States. They were not physically attractive people and contemporary reports would have us believe that they were not particularly brave in battle. It appears that the Atakapans summered on the coast and wintered some distance inland. Archeological finds west of Houston, near Addicks, give evidence of their presence. The northernmost members of the tribe gardened and hunted and fished as the Caddo did. Along the coast, they took on the characteristics of the Karankawa, making wide use of shellfish and fish, utilizing dugout canoes and frequenting the barrier islands. They possessed some horses and hunted buffalo on occasion, traveling some distance inland to the herds. In the 1830s it was noted that they killed a great many deer.

Oddly enough, this timid, seemingly insignificant group of people are reported to have acted as conduits for the French, forwarding firearms to the Lipan Apaches to aid them in their wars against the Spaniards. Still, as an identifiable tribe, the Atakapans were never easy to delineate, and now that they are gone, it is impossible to say when they went—much less where they went. Most likely disease had much to do with their demise—germs and viruses took more Indian lives than bullets. Some scholars think that they moved out of their infected villages to join other bands. The most accepted thesis is that they were gone well before 1850 and their descendants, if indeed there are any, could be living on the Alabama-Coushatta Reservation near Woodville today, the only true native Texans.

South of the Atakapans lived the Karankawas who, though they owned some horses, retained their ancient ways in the marshes and on the barrier islands. They were considered dangerous by encroaching settlers, because they attacked in a random and unpredictable fashion. In more than one instance they killed part of a party and then escorted the survivors to their destination peacefully. It was the Karankawas who harassed San Felipe de Austin to the point that Stephen F. Austin hired ten young men to be paid from his own pocket and dubbed them Rangers. Texas Ranger historians point to this event as the birth of the organization.

At the request of the Karankawas, the Spaniards established several missions in their territory, but they proved impossible to "reduce," as the Spaniards termed it. The "Cronk," as they came to be called, tried politics too, offering to join first one side and then the other during the Texas Revolution in an effort to improve their standing. They met understandable resistance on both sides.

Finally, their ranks decimated by disease and warfare, the Karankawas sought refuge where they thought they could best find it, moving down the coast to Mexico early in the 1840s. They were pursued there also, and in 1858 a band fleeing soldiers in Mexico crossed the Rio Grande where they were wiped out by a group of Texas ranchers. Isaac Duval, a twenty-year-old scout for one of the many "peace commissions" of the new Republic of Texas who worked to bring as many Indian leaders as possible to a peace conference in 1845, reports making contact with a remnant band of Karankawas on the lower Pecos River, 300 miles from their former range. Though they agreed to come to the talks, it is not recorded that they did so.

Descriptions of the Texas Hill Country as late as the 1830s say that the grass grew stirrup high across the wide and open valleys. Watered by bubbling springs that still flow and creeks that still lace the rolling hills, the territory of the Tonkawas was a veritable paradise. Thus, when the Tonkawas obtained the horse, their relatively easy existence became even easier, making big game hunting less of an effort and moving from favored place to favored place less of a chore. It was the Tonkawas bad luck to have as neighbors the Apaches to the southwest, the Comanches to the west and north and the ever-increasing numbers of Spanish and Anglo-American settlers to the south and east. Surrounded by enemy groups, the Tonkawas took the only remaining road; they became scouts for the Mexicans and then the Anglo-Americans in their wars of attrition against the Apaches and Comanches. The "Tonks" were good horsemen and in time became expert trackers who knew the features of the hills and canyons of Central and South Texas. By the mid-1800s they were at the beck and call of the settler's posses and the scouting parties of the Texas Rangers. Sometime before the end of the nineteenth century, the Tonkawas, never very numerous to begin with, ceased to exist as a tribe.

The same fate befell the centuries-old line of the Coahuiltecans in Texas. They asked only to be left in peace. Instead, they were besieged by a steady stream of friars and priests looking to Christianize them, as well as hostile Indian neighbors attacking from every direction. They took refuge in the missions, not because they heard the spritual call, but because the mission walls were uniformly tall and comfortably thick. Unwilling, or unable, to adapt to the new technology of the horse, they slowly but surely were absorbed into the Mexican population and by 1850 had disappeared as Indians.

Events on the faraway Atlantic coast also had an effect on the Texas aborigines. The westward expansion that began after the Revolutionary War intensified after the War of 1812. Indians from the eastern seaboard, dispossessed of their lands, moved toward the sunset looking for some place to call home. The Choctaws and Chickasaws came into Texas from Mississippi and Georgia. The Creeks left Alabama and Georgia not long after the the Coushattas and the Alabamas fled the same area. The Kickapoos and Potawatomi left Illinois, and after stops in Missouri and Arkansas, made it to Texas. The Delawares ended their long journey with a last long trip from Missouri, as did the Shawnees. The Quapaws came from Arkansas. The Cherokees were badgered, persecuted and finally chased out of the southern Appalachians in Georgia and shoved across the Mississippi. The Seminoles fled Florida without ever surrendering to the American military. By 1800 representatives of the Shawnee, Delaware, Kickapoo, Seminole, Cherokee and other tribes had settled in at the headwaters of the Sabine among the last of the Caddos.

Life for Texas's aborigines in the years 1600 to 1836 was a series of wrenching changes and cataclysmic events. Up from the south came the Spaniards with horses and missionaries. The French showed up in the east, not to convert, but looking to do business by introducing firearms and giving the Spaniards cause to enter the country in force. Both brought diseases that the immune systems of the natives were unable to combat.

Once the horse culture had begun to spread, the Apaches dealt out their own brand of misery to the weaker tribes. The Apaches, in turn, found out what life was like on the other end of the lance as the Comanches chased them off the best of the range and into exile. Hard on the Comanche's heels, but from the opposite direction, came Indian refugees and right behind them, their enemies, the Anglo-Americans.

As 1830 dawned, the Indian groups of Texas were beginning to disintegrate. The Jumanos were, for all practical purposes, extinct. The Caddos, declining at the beginning of the era were now badly decimated, though their ranks had swelled some by resettled southeastern natives. The Atakapans were all but gone, as were the resiliant Karankawas, and the Coahuiltecans were fading into the Mexican population like a shadow at dusk. Hanging on by a thread, the Tonkawas hoped against hope that the new settlers from the east, these Anglos, would be the allies and friends that they had been looking for these past three hundred years.

And on the morning of April 22, 1836, the day after the Battle of San Jacinto, the fires around the Mexican prisoners were burning down. The cool grey light of dawn defined the 600 bodies of Santa Anna's best troops laying strewn across McCormick's Pasture and half submerged in Peggy's Lake on the banks of the San Jacinto River. The day after the most famous event in Texas history the last and bloodiest era in the history of the American Indian in Texas began.

INDIANS IN TEXAS
1830

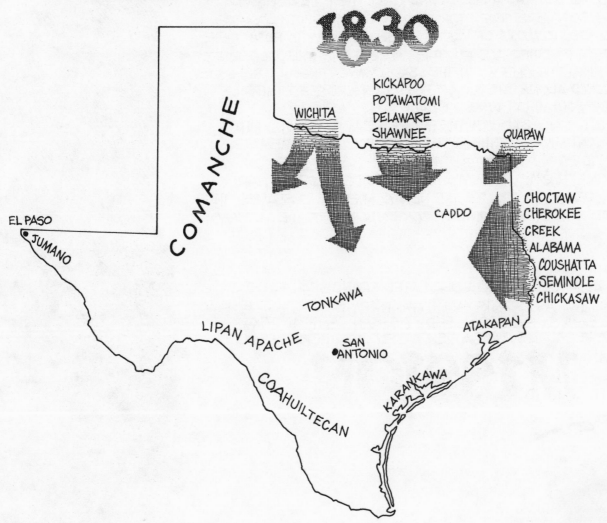

WHEN THE EUROPEANS CAME TO STAY IN THE AMERICAS THEY BROUGHT THEIR OWN VARIED WAYS AND MEANS OF DEALING WITH THE INDIANS THEY FOUND ON THE LAND.

THE ENGLISH TOOK WHAT THEY WANTED AND DEPENDED ON FORCE OF ARMS TO HOLD IT.

THE PRAGMATIC DUTCH HONORED THE PEOPLE ALREADY IN RESIDENCE BY NEGOTIATING AND PAYING FOR MOST OF THE LAND THEY SETTLED.

THE FRENCH CAME FOR FURS—IN THE MAIN—TRADING FOR THEM WITH BEADS AND TOOLS AND FIREARMS AND MAKING FEW DEMANDS ON THE PEOPLE OR THE LAND.

THE SPANISH CAME TO CONQUER. THEY FOUND GOLD IN MEXICO AND CENTRAL AMERICA AND ONCE THEY WERE FIRMLY ENSCONCED THERE THEY TURNED NORTH AND SOUTH LOOKING FOR MORE. RUMORS OF VAST RICHES LED THEM TO PUSH THEIR OUTPOSTS FURTHER AND FURTHER NORTH INTO THE WILDERNESS.

WITH THE CLERGY IN THE LEAD, CONVERTING ALL THE SOULS THEY COULD ALONG THE WAY, THEY SOON CROSSED THE RIO GRANDE INTO WHAT WOULD BECOME TEXAS.

IN CONCERT WITH THE PADRES CAME THE MILITARY, REPRESENTATIVES OF THE CROWN AND THE CLERGYMEN'S PROTECTORS THOUGH OFTEN, THE TWO WERE NOT EVEN ON SPEAKING TERMS. THE MILITARY ALSO DEVELOPED—EARLY ON—A TENDENCY TO USE THE NEW CONVERTS AS SLAVES. THIS BECAME A REGULAR POINT OF CONTENTION WITH THE CLERGY.

IN APRIL OF 1729, A DEDICATED FRANCISCAN FATHER WITH HIS TWO ASSISTANTS AND HIS MILITARY ESCORT MAKE CAMP ON THE BANKS OF A SPRING FED CREEK IN CENTRAL TEXAS. HERE THE PADRE WILL GATHER HIS FLOCK... HERE HE WILL BUILD HIS **MISSION**

THE FIRST ORDER OF BUSINESS IS A SHELTER FOR THE CROSS AND A SIX FOOT TALL STATUE OF ST. FRANCIS THAT HAS BEEN CARRIED OVER THE TRACKLESS LANDSCAPE FROM SALTILLO.

AT THE OUTSET THE LOCAL COAHUILTECANS WERE SHY AND FEARFUL OF THESE OUTSIDERS WHO LOOKED AND ACTED SO STRANGELY, BUT AS WITH PEACEFUL INVASIONS THROUGHOUT HISTORY, SUGAR CONES AND CHOCOLATE BARS MADE THE FIRST FEW STEPS EASIER.

BY MID-NOVEMBER WHEN THE FIRST BLUE NORTHER ROARED DOWN FROM THE HILLS, CRUDE SHELTERS WERE READY FOR THE SOLDIERS AND A REGULAR CONTINGENT OF FORTY-TWO INDIANS WERE IN PERMANENT CAMP NEARBY.

THE SOLDIERS' QUARTERS HAD BEEN BUILT WITH THE HELP OF THE INDIANS, CYNICALLY BRIBED BY THE MILITARY MEN INTO DOING THE HEAVIEST AND DIRTIEST OF THE LABOR. THE PADRE BASKED IN HIS SUCCESS AT GETTING ALL OF THE ADULT INDIANS TO ACCEPT THE UNIVERSAL CHURCH AND ESPECIALLY, NEVER MISSING COMMUNION. HIS MOOD TURNED GREY THOUGH WHEN HE THOUGHT OF THE COMING WINTER AND THE PROBLEMS HE FORESAW KEEPING THE BACHELOR SOLDIERS WITH TOO LITTLE TO DO, APART FROM THE INDIAN WOMEN.

MARCH, 1730—THE PADRE HAS SPENT THE PAST TEN MONTHS STUDYING THE LAY OF THE LAND AND NOW, WITH THE DAYS GROWING WARMER, HE HAS MADE HIS DECISION.

A LOW RISE ON THE EAST SIDE OF THE CREEK A HALF MILE BELOW THE PRESIDIO IS THE SPOT HE'S CHOSEN FOR HIS MISSION. WITH HIS NEW CONVERTS GATHERED ABOUT HIM HE BLESSES THE SITE IN HIS MORNING PRAYERS.

THEY WILL BEGIN WITH THE GRANARY. THE HARVEST FROM THE SEED THEY WILL SOON PLANT WILL NEED TO BE STORED.

JUNE, 1730—THE PROMISED SETTLERS ARRIVE! VOLUNTEERS FROM THE UNFORTUNATES OF MEXICO CITY, THEY HAVE BEEN PROMISED FREE LAND AND A NEW LIFE. THEY BRING WITH THEM ALL THAT THEY OWN—WHICH ISN'T MUCH—AND THE BREEDING STOCK TO BEGIN THE MISSION'S CATTLE HERD. ONE HUNDRED YEARS LATER THEIR DESCENDANTS WILL FURNISH THE RAW MATERIAL FOR TEXAS' CATTLE INDUSTRY.

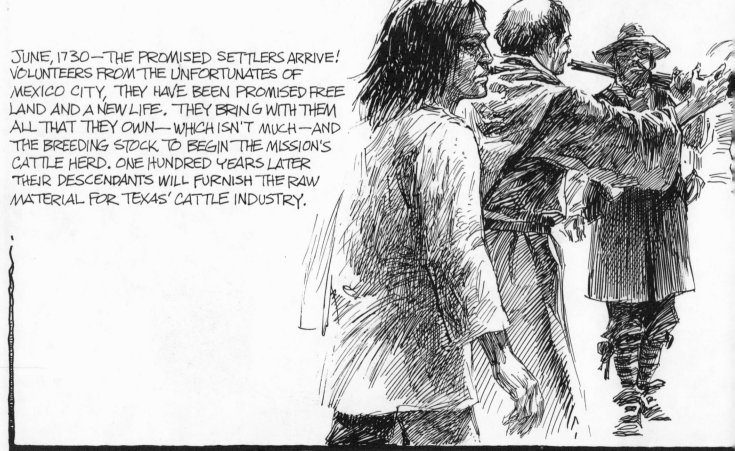

OCTOBER, 1743 — THERE IS STILL WORK TO DO ON THE GRIST MILL, BUT THE MISSION COMPOUND IS COMPLETE. THIS SUNDAY MORNING ALL ARE IN ATTENDANCE AT MASS FOR THE BLESSING OF THE MISSION AND AFTERWARDS, THE FIRST CHRISTIAN WEDDING WILL TAKE PLACE BETWEEN TWO YOUNG INDIANS.

IT IS A DAY FOR FEASTING AND CELEBRATION. DESPITE ALL OF THE ODDS AGAINST HIM, THE PADRE HAS SUCCEEDED. HE BROUGHT THE CHURCH INTO A WILDERNESS AND PLANTED A SEED SO STRONG THAT IT SURVIVED HEAT AND COLD, INTERNAL STRIFE CAUSED BY THE MILITARY, THE UNEXPLAINED COMINGS AND GOINGS OF THE MISSION INDIANS AND PERIODIC ATTACKS BY HOSTILE APACHES, THE ENDLESS SQUABBLES IN THE VILLAGE AND THE DAILY DRUDGERY OF ALMOST FOURTEEN YEARS OF CONSTANT CONSTRUCTION.

THROUGH IT ALL THE PADRE HAS STAYED THE COURSE AND KEPT THE FAITH. HIS INDIAN CHARGES NOW NUMBER 342 — THOUGH THE NUMBER IS ALWAYS HIGHER AS WINTER APPROACHES. THE CIVILIAN POPULATION HAS GROWN TO 106 AND IT CONTINUES TO PROSPER IN SPITE OF ITSELF. THE GARRISON NUMBERS 150, THEIR NUMBER SWELLING TO 320 WHEN MARRIED SOLDIERS' DEPENDENTS ARE INCLUDED.

IN THIS WILDERNESS OCEAN, THEY HAVE BUILT AN ISLAND OF CIVILIZATION.

FOR THE COAHUILTECAN IT IS AN ISLAND OF SAFETY AND STABILITY.

NOVEMBER, 1743 — TWENTY MILES SOUTHEAST A RANCHO HAS BEEN BUILT TO SHELTER THE MISSION'S STOCK HANDLERS. THEY ARE ASSIGNED BY THE PADRE ON A ROTATING BASIS FOR THIS IS A LONELY PLACE TO STAY FOR LONG AND AT TIMES IT IS A HAZARDOUS PLACE TO SAY THE LEAST. THE WALLS OF THE HOUSE ARE OF ROCK, THREE FEET THICK. THERE ARE NO WINDOWS, ONLY GUN PORTS.

THERE IS NO DANGER OF APACHE ATTACK NOW. WITH THE ROUND-UP AND BRANDING GOING ON FOR THE NEXT THREE WEEKS UPWARDS OF 100 VAQUEROS, INDIANS AND SOLDIERS WILL BE COMING AND GOING.

BACK AT THE MISSION THE GRANARY IS FULL TO OVERFLOWING AS THE FINISHING TOUCHES ARE PUT ON THE HARVEST. EXPERIENCE HAS SHOWN THAT THE WET, COLD WINTER WILL BE ALONG SOON.

WHEN WINTER SETS IN WITH IT'S BONE CHILLING COLD THE MISSION DOES NOT HIBERNATE. ALL HANDS TURN TO THE THINGS THAT WERE PUT ASIDE DURING THE BUSY SUMMER. SPINNING, WEAVING, SEWING, CANDLE AND SOAP MAKING AND A HUNDRED OTHER CHORES WILL MORE THAN FILL THEIR TIME UNTIL, ONCE AGAIN, THE PLANTING SEASON ARRIVES.

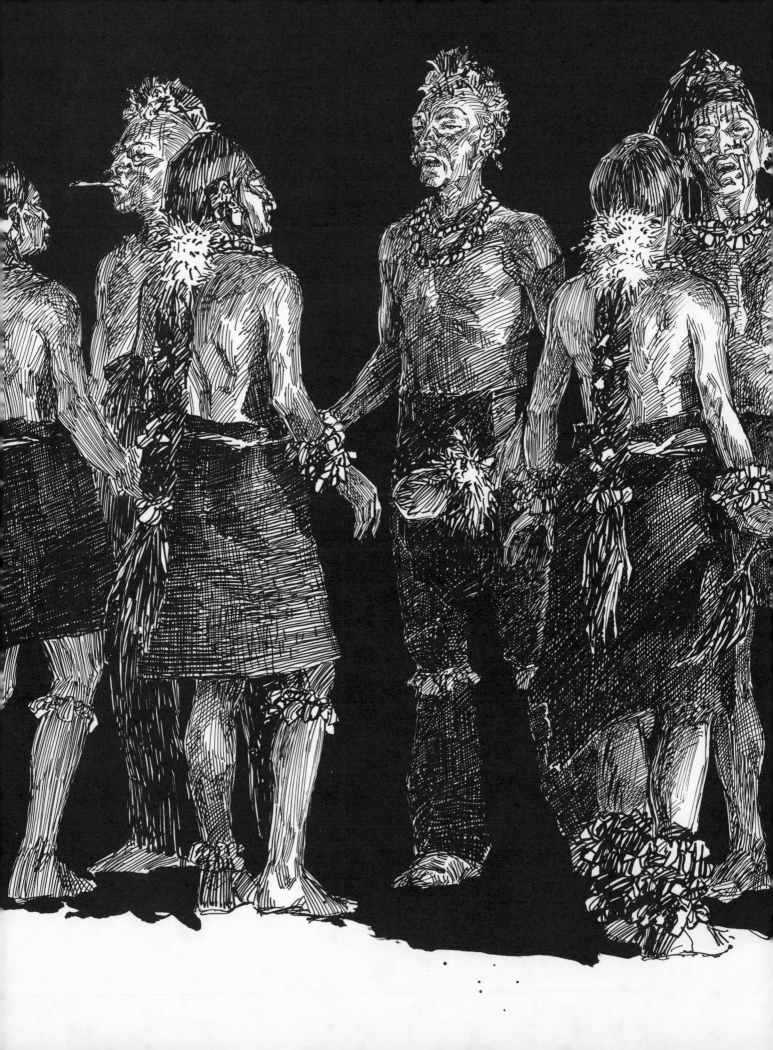

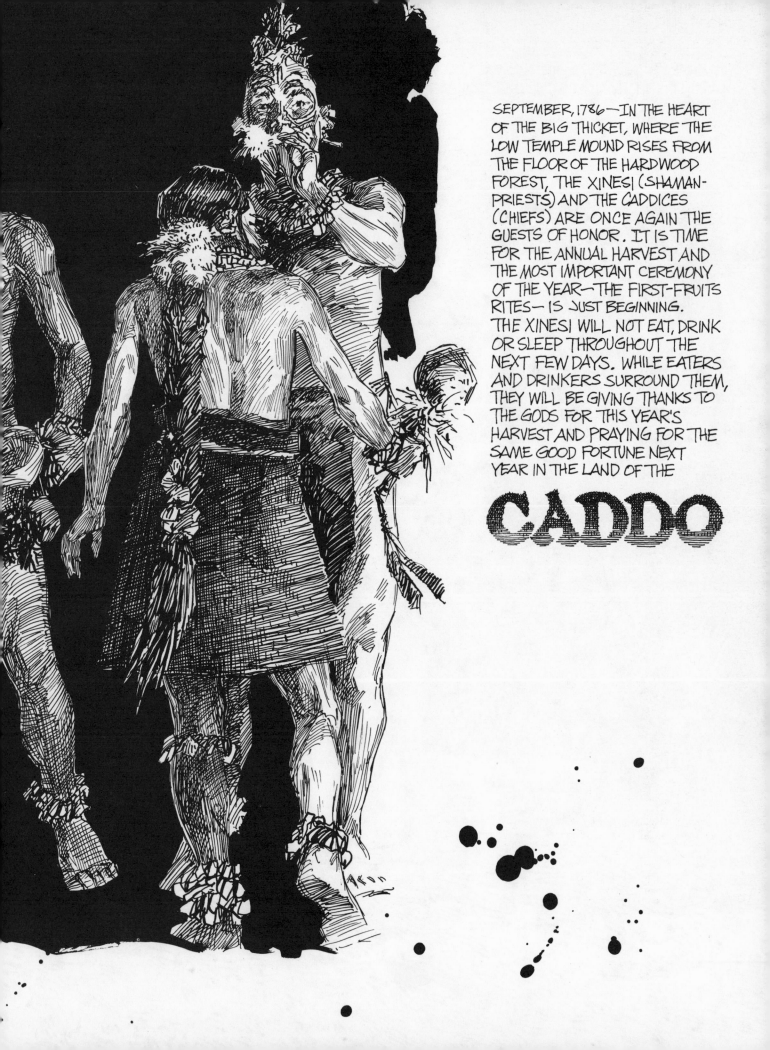

SEPTEMBER, 1786—IN THE HEART OF THE BIG THICKET, WHERE THE LOW TEMPLE MOUND RISES FROM THE FLOOR OF THE HARDWOOD FOREST, THE XINESI (SHAMAN-PRIESTS) AND THE CADDICES (CHIEFS) ARE ONCE AGAIN THE GUESTS OF HONOR. IT IS TIME FOR THE ANNUAL HARVEST AND THE MOST IMPORTANT CEREMONY OF THE YEAR—THE FIRST-FRUITS RITES—IS JUST BEGINNING. THE XINESI WILL NOT EAT, DRINK OR SLEEP THROUGHOUT THE NEXT FEW DAYS. WHILE EATERS AND DRINKERS SURROUND THEM, THEY WILL BE GIVING THANKS TO THE GODS FOR THIS YEAR'S HARVEST AND PRAYING FOR THE SAME GOOD FORTUNE NEXT YEAR IN THE LAND OF THE

CADDO

IN THE SPRING, ALL THE MEN AND WOMEN HAD GATHERED IN THE LOWLAND FIELDS. BEGINNING WITH THE CHIEF'S FIELD, THE ENTIRE COMMUNITY WORKED UNTIL EVERY PLOT WAS TILLED AND PLANTED WITH TWO KINDS OF CORN, SQUASH, FIVE VARIETIES OF BEANS, SUNFLOWERS AND TOBACCO.

IN THE RICH EAST TEXAS SOIL, MINIMUM CARE USUALLY PRODUCED FINE RESULTS AND THE CADDO ALMOST NEVER WENT HUNGRY.

THEY LIVED IN THE MIDST OF NATURAL ABUNDANCE IN THE WOODS AND STREAMS, SUPPLEMENTING THEIR GARDEN PRODUCE WITH DEER, FISH AND BUFFALO...

...AND TAKING FULL ADVANTAGE OF THE WILD FRUITS AND NUTS THAT RIPENED AROUND THEM.

BECAUSE GATHERING FOOD TOOK UP SO LITTLE OF THEIR TIME, LIFE IN THE CADDO VILLAGES AND HAMLETS TOOK ON A TEXTURE UNKNOWN AMONG OTHER TEXAS INDIANS. THEY ELECTED OFFICIALS TO PERFORM SPECIFIC DUTIES AND EXPECTED THEM TO DEVOTE FULL TIME TO THEIR WORK. THEY DEVELOPED CRAFTS LIKE WEAVING AND POTTERY TO A LEVEL THAT ASTONISHED THE EUROPEANS WHO FIRST VISITED THEM.

THEY WERE ALSO FORMIDABLE WARRIORS AND THEIR FEROCIOUSNESS—AT LEAST IN OPPONENT'S EYES—WAS PROBABLY ENHANCED BY THEIR PRACTICE OF TORTURING AND EATING THEIR CAPTIVES.

ALONG WITH POLITICAL ORGAN-
IZATION CAME AN EXQUISITELY
COMPLICATED RELIGION. THEY
CELEBRATED A WIDE ARRAY OF
FEAST DAYS, THE MAJOR ONES
TRIGGERED BY THE CHANGING
SEASONS. THE TEMPLE, ATOP
AN EARTHEN MOUND, WAS THE
FOCUS OF THE CADDOES
DAILY LIFE. INSIDE WAS KEPT
AN EVER BURNING FLAME.

WHILE THEIR SOCIETY WAS THE
MOST SOPHISTICATED OF ALL
TEXAS INDIANS, THEIR CLOSE
KNIT HAMLET-VILLAGE
STYLE OF LIVING WORKED
AGAINST THEM WHEN THEY
WERE ATTACKED BY THE
WHITE MAN'S DISEASES.

IN A COUNTRYSIDE FILLED WITH PREDATORS, IT'S A WONDER THEY'VE GOTTEN THIS FAR... THIS YOUNG MAN WHO GREW UP AN ORPHAN IN THE HACIENDAS SOUTH OF SAN ANTONIO AND THIS YOUNG WOMAN OF THE HIGHEST CLASS.

SHE HAD TAKEN NOTICE OF HIS KIND AND GENTLE MANNER AND HIS SHY SMILE EARLY ON AND HE — HE HAD THOUGHT OF NO ONE BUT HER FOR AS LONG AS HE COULD REMEMBER.

HER FATHER WOULD NOT HAVE THIS UNION. IN THEIR HIGHLY STRUCTURED SOCIETY HE COULD NOT ALLOW HER TO MARRY BELOW HER STATION, EVEN IF HE HAD TO KILL THE BOY TO PREVENT IT. THIS, HE PROMISED HER, HE WOULD DO AT THE FIRST OPPORTUNITY.

SO THEY TOOK FOUR HORSES FROM HER FATHER'S REMUDA AND IN THE DEAD HOURS OF A MOONLESS NIGHT, THEY RODE HARD TO THE NORTH AND EAST. THEY HAVE HEARD OF A PLACE CALLED NEW ORLEANS AND THERE, THEY ARE CERTAIN, THEY WILL BE SAFE. WHILE THE GIRL'S FRANTIC RELATIVES ARE SENDING MESSENGERS TO THE SOUTH AND EAST, BY DAWN THE TWO HAVE CROSSED CIBOLO CREEK AND ARE WELL ON THEIR WAY.

ON THE SECOND DAY THEY LOST ONE OF THEIR HORSES. ON THE THIRD DAY THEY CROSSED THE SAME RIVER THREE TIMES. ON THE FOURTH DAY THE SEASON'S FIRST BLUE NORTHER CAME DOWN ON THEM WITH IT'S CUTTING WINDS AND STINGING SLEET. BY THE AFTERNOON OF THE FIFTH DAY A SECOND HORSE WAS GONE AND WITH THE REMAINING TWO ANIMALS THEY ARE HUDDLED ON THE LEE SIDE OF A GROVE OF TREES. WITH THE TEMPERATURE CONTINUING TO DROP, WET AND CHILLED TO THE BONE AND UNABLE TO START A FIRE, THEY ARE VERY NEARLY FINISHED WHEN THEY ARE FOUND BY A HUNTING PARTY OF

TONKAWA

IT TAKES A WHILE TO CONVINCE THE TWO THAT THEY MEAN NO HARM, BUT
WHEN THEY ARE FINALLY UNDERSTOOD, THE THREE INDIANS MOUNT THE
COUPLE ON THEIR OWN HORSES AND TAKING THE OTHER TWO ANIMALS
IN TOW, THEY HEAD TO THE NORTHWEST, FACE TO THE STORM.
FROM LONG EXPERIENCE WITH NORTHERS, THE TONKAWAS
KNOW THAT THERE IS NO TIME TO WASTE IF THESE TWO
ARE TO LIVE THROUGH THE NIGHT.

CAMPED AMONG A STAND OF LIVE OAKS UP A SHORT HILL FROM FRESH WATER, THE TONKAWAS ARE WELL PREPARED FOR THE UNPREDICTABLE WINTER WEATHER.

IN SHORT ORDER, THE COUPLE IS TAKEN INSIDE AND TURNED OVER TO THE WOMEN. THEY STRIP THE WET CLOTHING FROM THE TWO AND, TAKING OFF THEIR OWN, THEY CRAWL UNDER THE BUFFALO ROBES TO WARM THEM WITH THE HEAT OF THEIR OWN BODIES.

BY MORNING THE GIRL IS REVIVED BUT
THE YOUNG MAN IS NOT AT ALL WELL AND
THE INDIAN WOMEN BREW A SOUP OF
WILD ONION AND PEPPERS AND
PEMMICAN. HE MUST EAT
SOMETHING AND THOUGH HE
COMPLAINS OF THE COLD,
HIS SKIN FEELS OF FIRE.

THE GIRL WATCHES OVER HIM THROUGH THE DAY. THAT NIGHT, IN HER PRAYERS, HIS LIFE IS ALL THAT SHE ASKS FOR.

THE SPIRITS THAT HAVE INVADED THE YOUNG MAN'S BODY TALK AND MOAN THROUGH THE NIGHT AND BY MORNING THE SHAMAN IS SENT FOR. HE SPENDS THE BETTER PART OF THE DAY CALLING THE EVIL OUT OF THE SICK BOY AND BY SUNSET, THEY CAN DO NOTHING MORE THAN WAIT TO SEE IF HIS POWERS ARE ENOUGH.

ONCE AGAIN HE PROVES HIS MASTERY OVER THE DEMONS. IN THE MIDDLE OF THE NIGHT THE YOUNG MAN CALLS FOR WATER, WHICH THE WOMEN RUSH HAPPILY TO PROVIDE.

WITH THE FEVER BROKEN, THE YOUNG MAN QUICKLY REGAINED HIS STRENGTH. THOUGH THE TWO DID NOT BELIEVE ANYONE WOULD LOOK FOR THEM IN A TONKAWA CAMP, THEY WERE ANXIOUS TO BE ON THEIR WAY.

THE THREE MEN WHO FOUND THEM HALF-FROZEN UNDER THE TREES TEN DAYS AGO LEFT WITH THEM. THEY, TOO, HAD HEARD RUMORS OF THE VILLAGE CALLED NEW ORLEANS, AND THEY KNEW FOR CERTAIN OF SETTLEMENTS TO THE EAST. THEY GUIDED THEM THIS WAY.

THEY PARTED COMPANY AT THE SAN BERNARD, THE INDIANS WATCHING THE PAIR CROSS OVER TO THE EAST BANK AND LINGERING UNTIL THEY WERE OUT OF SIGHT IN THE TREES.

THE YOUNG MAN AND THE GIRL, CARED FOR BY THE TONKAWA AND SENT ON THEIR WAY WITH FOOD AND WARM ROBES, WOULD REACH THEIR DESTINATION ON THE EVENING OF OCTOBER 20, 1803 — THE VERY DAY THAT THE SENATE OF THE UNITED STATES RATIFIED THE LOUISIANA PURCHASE.

THE TONKAWAS RETURNED TO THEIR CAMP AND THEIR FAMILIES, WHERE THEY WOULD LIVE AS THEY HAD FOR CENTURIES FOR JUST A LITTLE WHILE LONGER.

THE GRANDMOTHER SITS DOWN STIFFLY ON THE SAND. THE ARTHRITIS THAT HAS LONG SINCE SETTLED INTO NEARLY EVERY JOINT MAKES ANY ACTION A MAJOR AND PAINFUL EFFORT.

AS SHE WATCHES THE LITTLE BAND OF

KARANKAWA

GATHER THEIR FEW RUDE PERSONAL BELONGINGS, HER THOUGHTS CARRY HER BACK TO HER YOUTH WHEN HER PEOPLE ROAMED FREE OVER THE BROAD COASTAL PLAIN.

THOSE WERE WONDERFUL DAYS INDEED. THE BAYS WERE FULL OF FISH AND OYSTERS, THE OYSTERS FULLY AS BIG AS HER HAND.

THEY SPENT THE HOTTEST DAYS IN THE SURF OR WADING THE BAY WATERS. ON THE LAKES JUST A SHORT WALK INLAND, WATER BIRDS WERE PLENTIFUL, ESPECIALLY AT SUMMER'S END. SHE COULD ALMOST FEEL THE MOTION OF THE DUGOUT CANOE AS HER FATHER POLED IT THROUGH THE MAZE OF OPEN CHANNELS IN THE TIDAL FLATS. SHE SMILES AT THE THOUGHT OF THE RIPENED TUNAS THEY GATHERED FROM THE PRICKLY PEARS.

SHE'S BEEN WONDERING THESE PAST FEW YEARS ABOUT THE BERRIES AND GRAPES. THEY HAVEN'T BEEN SO NUMEROUS SINCE THE WHITE MEN STARTED COMING AND THE BEE TREES ARE HARDER TO FIND.

THE SPANISH AND THE FRENCH WEREN'T SO BAD. THE FRENCH CAME WITH GOODS TO TRADE, THINGS SHE COULD USE LIKE HER GOOD IRON POT. SHE MISSED THAT POT.

THE SPANISH WERE VERY STRANGE, WITH THEIR SHAMANS ALL WRAPPED IN CLOTH. AND THEY SMELLED BAD.

BUT AT LEAST THEY WENT AWAY — NOT LIKE THESE WHITE MEN.

SHE REMEMBERS THE STORY, HOW LONG YEARS AGO, SOME OTHER WHITE MEN HAD COME OUT OF THE BIG WATER. THEY WERE THE FIRST THEY HAD EVER SEEN, THESE MEN WITH SKIN THE COLOR OF A FLOUNDER'S BELLY. THERE WAS ONE OF THEM WHO WAS BLACK ALL OVER, WITH HAIR LIKE THE MOSS IN THE OAK TREES. ALL VERY STRANGE.

THEY WERE GODS OF SOME SORT WHO DIDN'T REVEAL THEIR MAGIC UNTIL MUCH LATER. PERHAPS THE TRIALS THAT HER PEOPLE WERE GOING THROUGH THESE PAST YEARS WERE PUNISHMENT FOR THE WAY THESE GODS WERE FIRST TREATED.

BUT WHAT WERE HER PEOPLE TO DO? THEY LATER CAME ON THE GRISLY EVIDENCE OF THE CANNIBALISM OF FOUR OF THE WHITE MEN BY ANOTHER OF THEIR NUMBER.

SHE REMEMBERS WHEN JEAN LAFITTE'S PIRATES ON GALVESTON ISLAND STOLE THE WIFE OF HER COUSIN. THEY TRIED NOT TO HAVE ANYTHING TO DO WITH THESE MEN, FOR THEY WERE A DANGEROUS BAND. THEY ALL CARRIED LONG KNIVES AND AT LEAST ONE GUN.

AROUND THE BIG HOUSE THEY HAD BUILT ON THE ISLAND, WITH THE SMALLER HUTS AROUND IT, THERE WAS ALWAYS SOME SORT OF COMMOTION GOING ON.

THEY HAD A LOT OF THE BLACK PEOPLE THERE TOO, BUT THEY WERE TREATED LIKE SHE WOULD NEVER STAND TO BE TREATED, TIED UP IN CAGES

UNTIL SOMEONE WOULD TAKE THEM AWAY. SHE HAD HEARD THAT THEY WERE TRADED FOR THE HARD YELLOW METAL THE WHITE MEN THOUGHT SO MUCH OF.

WHEN HER COUSIN AND HIS FRIENDS WENT TO GET HIS WIFE BACK, THE WHITE MEN WOULDN'T LET HER GO. SO HER COUSIN KILLED ONE OF THE

MEN AND HIS FRIENDS KILLED SOME OTHERS. THEY BROUGHT HIS WIFE BACK, FOR THEIR SMALL SON WAS HUNGRY AND CRYING AND SHE WAS NEEDED.

THAT NIGHT, AS THEY ALL SLEPT, THE WHITE MEN ATTACKED WITH THEIR TWO CANNONS.

BY THE TIME THE WHITES HAD LEFT, THIRTY KARANKAWAS LAY DEAD. SHE HAD NEVER SEEN SUCH WANTON DESTRUCTION.

THE NEXT MORNING, HER OLDEST SON DIED OF HIS WOUNDS. SHE HERSELF STILL CARRIED A PIECE OF METAL FIRED FROM A CANNON. THAT'S

PROBABLY WHY HER SHOULDER ACHED SO WHEN THE COLD AND THE RAINS CAME.

THE THOUGHT OF THE SON WHO DIED HURT IN A DIFFERENT WAY.

THE REAL TROUBLE CAME WHEN THE LITTLE CHIEF, THE ONE CALLED AUSTIN, CAME WITH HIS BAND AND THEY BUILT THEIR WOODEN HOUSES UP THE RIVER. THAT BAND WAS VERY RICH, WITH ALL OF THEIR HORSES AND CATTLE AND THOSE LITTLE BIRDS THAT THEY KEPT IN THEIR YARDS.

THEY HAD SO MUCH THAT IT WAS HARD TO BELIEVE THAT THEY WOULD FIGHT TO THE POINT OF BEING KILLED THEMSELVES TO KEEP THE INDIANS FROM TAKING A LITTLE.

AFTER ALL, HADN'T HER PEOPLE LEFT THEM ALONE WHEN THEY CAME TO THE BAYS AND GATHERED BARRELS FULL OF OYSTERS AND FISH, TAKING IT ALL AWAY IN THEIR WAGONS? AND WEREN'T THE PEOPLE WILLING TO SHARE THEIR DUCKS AND GEESE WITH THEM?

IT WAS HARD TO BELIEVE THAT THEY WOULD FIGHT SO HARD OVER SUCH SMALL THINGS AS A HORSE OR COW, AND HARDER YET TO IMAGINE THAT THEY WOULD GET TOGETHER WITH THE SPANIARDS. ON THAT HORRIBLE AFTERNOON, THEY DROVE THE KARANKAWA INTO MATAGORDA BAY AND KILLED FULLY HALF THEIR NUMBER.

SHE WAS NOT THERE, BUT SHE HEARD THE WHOLE STORY LATER.

THEN THE SPANIARDS STARTED TO CALL THEMSELVES MEXICANS, AND NOT LONG AFTER THAT, THEY STARTED TO FIGHT THE WHITE MEN. THEY WERE SO BUSY FIGHTING EACH OTHER THAT THEY LEFT THE KARANKAWA ALONE.

THE LEADERS OF THE PEOPLE, IN COUNCIL, DECIDED THAT THEY COULD GAIN THE FAVOR OF THE NEW AND STRONGER PEOPLE IF THEY FOUGHT ON THEIR SIDE. THEY WERE NOT FOOLS THOUGH. THEY HAD BEEN TRADING FOR SOME OF THE GOOD THINGS THAT THE WHITE MEN HAD LIKE SHIRTS AND THE BIG WIDE BRIMMED HATS THAT KEPT THE SUN FROM BEING SO HOT ON THEIR HEADS.

SO THEY WERE CAREFUL TO WEAR ONLY WHAT THEY HAD GOTTEN FROM THE SPANISH WHEN THEY WENT TO SEE THE MEXICANS...

AND WORE ONLY WHAT THEY HAD GOTTEN FROM THE WHITE MEN WHEN THEY WENT TO SEE THEM.

SHE COULD NOT UNDERSTAND WHY THEIR OFFER TO FIGHT HAD BEEN REJECTED BY BOTH SIDES, FOR THE MEN OF HER PEOPLE WERE VERY BRAVE WARRIORS WITH STRONG MEDICINE.

THEY WENT BACK TO THE BAYS WHERE THE TROUT WERE COMING IN EARLY THAT YEAR AND WERE SO THICK THAT THEY COULD BE CAUGHT IN THE SHALLOW WATER WITH BARE HANDS.

HER ONLY GRANDSON WAS FOUR YEARS OLD THAT SPRING, AND IT WAS HER GREAT PLEASURE TO WATCH AS HE BEGAN TO LEARN THE WAYS OF THE PEOPLE.

NOW THE WHITE MEN HAVE BEATEN THE MEXICANS AND ARE COMING INTO THE COUNTRY IN NUMBERS TOO GREAT TO COUNT. THEIR HOUSES ARE EVERY-WHERE, AND SOME OF THEM WILL SHOOT AT THE PEOPLE WHENEVER THEY SEE THEM. ALL OF THE WHITE MEN RIDE HORSES AND A KARANKA-WA CAUGHT IN THE OPEN IS AS GOOD AS DEAD.

THERE IS NO PLACE FOR THEM TO LIVE NOW. THE GREAT PRICKLY PEAR FIELD THAT SHE HAD VISITED EVERY FALL OF HER LIFE HAS BEEN BURNED OFF AND PLANTED IN COTTON. THE WHITE MEN ARE CHASING THE GAME AWAY JUST BY BEING ON THE LAND—THEY MAKE SO MUCH NOISE.

SHE COULD NOT UNDERSTAND WHY THEIR OFFER TO FIGHT HAD BEEN REJECTED BY BOTH SIDES, FOR THE MEN OF HER PEOPLE WERE VERY BRAVE WARRIORS WITH STRONG MEDICINE.

THEY WENT BACK TO THE BAYS WHERE THE TROUT WERE COMING IN EARLY THAT YEAR AND WERE SO THICK THAT THEY COULD BE CAUGHT IN THE SHALLOW WATER WITH BARE HANDS.

HER ONLY GRANDSON WAS FOUR YEARS OLD THAT SPRING, AND IT WAS HER GREAT PLEASURE TO WATCH AS HE BEGAN TO LEARN THE WAYS OF THE PEOPLE.

NOW THE WHITE MEN HAVE BEATEN THE MEXICANS AND ARE COMING INTO THE COUNTRY IN NUMBERS TOO GREAT TO COUNT. THEIR HOUSES ARE EVERYWHERE, AND SOME OF THEM WILL SHOOT AT THE PEOPLE WHENEVER THEY SEE THEM. ALL OF THE WHITE MEN RIDE HORSES AND A KARANKAWA CAUGHT IN THE OPEN IS AS GOOD AS DEAD.

THERE IS NO PLACE FOR THEM TO LIVE NOW. THE GREAT PRICKLY PEAR FIELD THAT SHE HAD VISITED EVERY FALL OF HER LIFE HAS BEEN BURNED OFF AND PLANTED IN COTTON. THE WHITE MEN ARE CHASING THE GAME AWAY JUST BY BEING ON THE LAND—THEY MAKE SO MUCH NOISE.

HER BAND HAS DECIDED TO GO SOUTH, AND THEY HAVE COME TO THE BIG WATER TO FOLLOW THE COASTLINE UNTIL THEY FIND A PLACE WHERE THE WHITE MEN ARE NOT.

THEY HAVE TRAVELED THREE DAYS NOW AND IT IS CLEAR THAT SHE WILL NOT BE ABLE TO GO THE REST OF THE WAY. SHE HAS GIVEN HER POSSESSIONS TO HER ONLY REMAINING DAUGHTER AND HAS HELD HER GRANDCHILDREN CLOSE FOR THE LAST TIME. SHE WILL SIT HERE ON THE BEACH AND WATCH THE BAND MOVE SOUTH UNTIL THEY ARE OUT OF SIGHT. AS THE TIDE COMES IN SHE WILL SING HER DEATH SONG AND WAIT FOR THE NIGHT AND THE COYOTES THAT COME TO PROWL THE DUNES.

BOOK THREE . . . 1837–1900

"If I could build a wall from the Red River to the Rio Grande, so high that no Indian could scale it, the White people would go crazy trying to devise means to get beyond it."

—Sam Houston,
president of the Republic of Texas

"The White man and the Red man cannot dwell in harmony together. Nature forbids it."

—Mirabeau B. Lamar,
president of the Republic of Texas

The story of the American Indian in Texas between 1836 and 1874 is in many ways the story of the end of the Comanches. By 1854 other Texas tribes had been summarily dealt with by the Anglo-Americans. No other tribe resisted so staunchly as did the Comanches. No other tribe fought so viciously over so long a time span as did the Comanches. The bitterest of the struggles repeatedly described in pioneer memoirs invariably involved Comanches. In the end, when the violent struggle was over, the Comanches had not surrendered. They had run out of food and horses.

A number of things happened as a result of the defeat of Santa Anna's troops at San Jacinto on the afternoon of April 21, 1836. The defeat paved the way for an avalanche of settlers from the United States. Indeed, thousands of land-hungry Anglo-Americans stood poised on the east bank of the Sabine River for most of the month of April awaiting the outcome of the Texas Revolution. And without the Mexican military threat, the new immigrants, and those already on the scene, were free to devote their full attention to the "Indian problem."

For their part, the Indians in Texas were perplexed. Indians had traditional enemies. Comanches fought Apaches just as their forefathers had done. Caddos and Wacos had always shot at each other on sight. They found this new concept of war one day and peace the next a baffling state of affairs. Further, now that Anglos were coming into Texas in wholesale lots, the Indians found their old enemies, the Mexicans, anxious to make friends in exchange for periodic raids against the new settlements. Other tribes, like the Karankawas, who had found the Spaniards and Mexicans hard to get along with but at least tolerable to some degree, were hounded and harassed by the newcomers until leaving their traditional lands was their only chance for survival.

The new Republic, busy with internal intrigues and trying desperately to operate without money, left Indian affairs to the local settlements. In 1837, Noah Smithwick went to live with the Comanches for a time for the purpose of making a treaty with them for the people of Bastrop. He was delegated the task because he was the only one who could speak the Comanche version of Spanish. His negotiations were successful, culminating in an agreement to cease hostilities. In his reminiscences (published in 1900), he claims not to remember the provisions of the treaty since, as he continues, neither party lived up to the pact anyway. Smithwick's mission was one of many as the newly arrived Anglo-Americans tried to secure their homes. They fast became tired of living in forts, barely subsisting on what they could grow while watching over their shoulders.

On the Indian side, the Comanches, in their treaty talks, insisted on a boundary, a dead-line, a place where settlement would stop and no white man would cross—a place where Indians would live in peace on one side and white men in peace on the other. The Anglo-Americans would agree to a dead-line, but they wanted one that the Indians would not cross but that they could. Rather than a dead-line, the two sides had a deadlock.

One of the more famous encounters between Texas Indians and white settlers occurred on May 19, 1836, when a band of Comanches, under the pretext of friendship, entered Parker's Fort near present-day Mexia. Once inside the compound, the Indians struck quickly, as was their practice, killing four men and a boy, wounding several others and taking five captives including nine-year-old Cynthia Ann Parker. All but Cynthia Ann were later returned. She lived with the Comanches for twenty-four years, became the wife of Peta Nocona, and bore him a daughter, Prairie Flower, and two sons, Pecos and Quanah. Texas Rangers, attacking a Comanche camp on the Pease River in 1860, "rescued" Cynthia Ann and Prairie Flower, but she was never happy back in the white world. Prairie Flower died soon after their rescue and by 1864 Cynthia Ann was dead also.

Sam Houston's dream of coexistence with the Indians was one he could never sell to a white population imbued with a "westward ho" tradition and a consuming hunger for land and riches. Repeated peace conferences ended with agreements of one sort or another but they were always negated by one more white settler moving onto Indian land or one more Indian band making a raid on the settlements.

The unsuccessful treaties can be blamed on the white man and the Indian alike, but a good part of the failure was due to simple ignorance and misunderstanding. Let us say, for example, that a treaty has been made between the settlers in Travis County and the local Indians. The month is May and the two parties assume that they will enjoy everlasting peace and good health as a result of this pact. Respecting the guidelines of that treaty several families move south to Hays County in time to set in their crops and build homes over the summer. In November, they are attacked by Indians because they are infringing upon the Indian's traditional wintering grounds. What the whites were so painfully slow to realize was that the Indian bands were just that—bands. Texas Indians, like almost all American Indian tribes, had no central political leader who could make and enforce agreements for all of the tribe. The attacking band in the example may have been five hundred miles away when the treaty was made and the Indians who signed the treaty were probably five hundred miles away in November.

In the usual course of events the Indians guilty of attacks were seldom caught outright, so punishment was meted out to the next bunch of Indians who came within range of the angry settlers. Neither band was guilty of breaking a treaty but both bands became the victim of mutual ignorance.

In 1839 Mirabeau B. Lamar was elected President of the Republic of Texas. In direct contrast to Sam Houston, who championed peaceful coexistence, Lamar advocated the removal or extermination of all Indians in Texas. His policy met with widespread public support and his first target was the hapless Cherokees who had settled in the vicinity of the Caddos in Northeast Texas. Charging that the Cherokees were in league with the Mexicans against the Anglo-Americans, Lamar ordered a campaign designed to drive the tribe out of the Republic.

The Cherokees present an interesting case in American Indian history. They were one of the few tribes who embraced the white man's ways. Traditional farmers from the southeastern states, they were quick to see the influx of Europeans as more than they could resist by force of arms. With extermination by the white man a serious possibility, they worked hard to appease him. They took up the white man's dress, the white man's religion and the white man's methods of farming. They moved into wooden houses and taught their children English. Sequoyah, a Cherokee, invented an alphabet for the Cherokee language and translated books of the Bible into Cherokee. But because they were Indians, they were denied clear title to their farm lands, which they tried in vain to acquire according to the white man's rules—land to which they had ancestral claim anyway. The majority of them were dispossessed of their farms and belongings and driven like so many cattle to the Indian Territory along the "Trail of Tears."

Some Cherokees entered Texas around 1800, and by 1839, when Lamar took office, they were trying once again to become good citizens in the white man's mold. Again they were frustrated in their attempts to gain title to the farms they worked. In July 1839, Lamar sent several regiments to drive the Cherokees from their lands. The Indians refused to go and in two battles on the 15th and 16th of the month, they were defeated. Chief Bowles, wearing a sash and sword that had been a gift from Sam Houston, was killed as he fought on foot after his horse was disabled. The remaining Cherokees were rounded up and pushed north across the Red River. Their farms, probably with crops already in the ground, and their livestock were taken by waiting white settlers. The Tonkawa Chief Placido and forty of his warriors fought on the side of the Texans.

In the following year, 1840, occurred one of the great debacles in Indian/white relations: the Council House Fight in San Antonio. During the winter of 1839–1840 the Comanches made contact with the leaders of San Antonio and asked for peace talks. The reply stated that talks could be arranged provided the Comanches returned any captives they held. On the morning of March 19, sixty-five Comanche men, women, and children entered San Antonio to parley with local authorities and with some state officials. Meeting in the Council House, the whites discovered that the Indians had brought in only one captive—a young girl named Matilda Lockhart—who had been with the tribe about two years. The Anglo-Americans asked again for the return of all captives, to which the Comanches replied that she was the only one. Matilda, however, said there were twelve others in a camp sixty miles away. The Anglo-Americans announced that they would hold the Indians in the Council House hostage until the other captives were brought in. To enforce the point they called in armed troops and Texas Rangers who had been kept in readiness nearby. Incensed by this turn of events the Comanches threw off their blankets and attacked. The end result was thirty-five dead Indian men, including all twelve chiefs who were present, and three women and children. Seven whites were killed and eight wounded. An Indian woman was sent to the Comanche camp with word that the remaining twenty-six Comanche were hostages and would be released when the twelve captives had been freed. For once, both sides kept their word.

The Comanches were enraged at what they regarded as a betrayal by the white men. They retreated to the plains where they gathered forces and on the morning of August 4, 1840, six hundred mounted Comanches led by Buffalo Hump appeared on the outskirts of Victoria. Without attacking the town proper they swept the area clean of horses and mules and any other stock they could find. A Mexican ranchero passing through town lost his entire herd of 500 horses.

As the citizens of Victoria huddled in the town square pondering their fate, the Comanches moved on toward the coast and to the little village of Linnville twenty-two miles away. The population of the town, about fifty people, retreated to a schooner anchored in Lavaca Bay, from which vantage point they watched as their town was destroyed. During the looting and burning of the town, the Comanches discovered a storehouse full of new clothing—top hats, frock coats, and fancy dresses—and a shipment of parasols. These garments struck their fancy, so their departure from Linnville was easily followed by watching the brightly colored parasols bobbing up and down as the Indians shaded themselves from the hot coastal sun.

John Linn, who recorded the incident in detail, says that the affair became too much for Judge John Hays, who took up a musket and waded ashore from the schooner for the express purpose of having at least one shot at the "red devils." He stood on the beach daring a Comanche, any Comanche, to come within range but—Linn surmised—the Indians imagined the judge was a "Big Medicine or something of the sort" and so steered clear of him. Hays, disgusted, finally returned to the schooner where it was discovered that the musket he had carried was not loaded. Such was the character of the protagonists on both sides.

After destroying Linnville and stripping the countryside of its livestock, this odd looking band of parasol carrying Comanches pushed up the north side of the Guadalupe River. Traveling now with more than one thousand horses and mules, they turned cross country for the Colorado. Near present-day Lockhart, on Plum Creek, they were met by a force of some four hundred Texas volunteers gathered by Ben McCulloch, and, in a running battle, the Comanches were thoroughly routed.

Armed mainly with bows and arrows, the Comanches sustained some 25–100 dead (depending on whose version of the battle you read) before making good their escape with about half the stock they had collected. The white men involved in the battle commandeered goods and stock that had been abandoned. Although the original owners could identify their property, the winners took the spoils. Linn tells of one Captain J. O. Wheeler who could point to his brand on 150 of the recaptured horses but was not allowed to reclaim his animals and had to ride home on a borrowed horse. Again, Placido and thirteen of his Tonkawas participated on the Texas side.

Determined to put an end to the Comanche raiding, President Lamar dispatched a force of one hundred men, along with twelve Lipan Apache scouts, up the Colorado some 300 miles to the Red Fork of that river, where a Comanche camp had been located. Attacking in the early morning, the Texans indiscriminately slaughtered 130 Indians, burned the village and returned with thirty-four women and children who were made slaves by the settlers. This was the worst defeat ever handed the Comanches by the Texans. It is not recorded if this was the camp of the Indians involved in the Linnville raid.

The entire Anglo-American area of the country was now under seige in a spiraling pattern of attack and retaliation. The fear and tension were instrumental in bringing an end to the Lamar administration and putting Sam Houston back in the president's office. Then began the long and slow process of trying to restore some semblance of peace to the frontier.

In the early 1800s, the remnants of the Caddos had settled on Sodo Creek, near present-day Shreveport, Louisiana. With the consummation of the Louisiana Purchase, they became wards of the United States, but as they were on the border with Mexican Texas, they found themselves courted by the Mexican government who wanted them as allies when the expected invasion from the United States took place. In 1835, with more and more United States citizens moving onto their range, the Caddos reached an agreement to sell their lands to the United States government and to cross the border to the west and resettle in Mexican Texas. Meanwhile, Mexico had been negotiating with the Caddos about setting aside land for them, negotiations made moot by the Texas Revolution. So the Caddos became, in effect, a people without a home. Treated harshly by Texans following Lamar's lead, they took up the arms and ammunition they had obtained from the United States when they sold their Louisiana land and began their own campaign of raids throughout North and East Texas. That is where things stood when Houston took the oath of office in 1841.

At Bird's Fort on the Trinity River, a treaty was signed on September 20, 1843 between Texas officials and the Caddo, Shawnee, Delaware, and some Wichita subtribes, the principal agreement being that peace between the Indians and the people of the Republic of Texas would last forever. The immigrant bands of Indians, the Delaware, Shawnee, Choctaw, Chickasaw and others, were not looked on with favor by the whites, except when they were recruited to chase down raiding Comanches. Now equipped with sophisticated weaponry these skilled hunters ventured onto the western plains in search of buffalo meat for their families and buffalo robes and hides, which could be exchanged for money and trade goods at posts throughout the frontier. The Comanches, still dependent upon the buffalo, viewed this new development with concern as they watched the great herds begin to dwindle before their eyes.

The immigrant Indians traveled with impunity through the plains, the Comanches not daring to face them in battle. The reason was simple. The immigrant Indians had new rifles of heavy caliber and long range, and they had enough ammunition to allow them to practice shooting. In contrast, "untamed" Indians either traded with Comancheros or acquired what firearms they owned as the spoils of war. In either case, they seldom had enough ammunition to be able to practice shooting, and often they carried the rifles into battle with only the round in the chamber available. Thus, circumstances forced these Indians to be only mediocre shots at best.

Desperate for peace in the west, Houston tried again, this time sending out a party under J. C. Eldridge in May 1843. In August the emissaries found a band of Penateka Comanches near present-day Lawton, Oklahoma. The Texas party, including a Waco chief and Delaware scouts, were made prisoners by the Comanches and, had it not been for the intervention of the Comanche chief, they would not have come back to report their failure. The Comanches had been betrayed one time too many.

Finally, after much effort, a group of Comanches and some members of smaller tribes were gathered at Council Springs, near present-day Mexia. A treaty was drawn up containing a clause concerning the long sought dead-line, but now Buffalo Hump did not like the placement of the line so it was stricken from the document. Once again promising everlasting peace, the document was signed and sealed by all parties, although they must have known at the time that the government of the Texas Republic was too weak and ineffectual to police such a list of do's and don'ts. The chiefs, for their part, certainly knew that any warrior who wanted to go on a raid was free to do so and to take as many of his fellows with him as wanted to follow.

So the troubles continued. One incident in 1845 involved a group of Delawares who killed a Comanche. The Comanches swore vengeance on the Delawares and their white friends and the fighting began anew. The continued killing of the buffalo for robes or hides only, leaving the carcass to the wolves and buzzards, only served to further aggravate matters.

In 1846 Texas became a state in the United States and the Indians became wards of the United States government. This development created new problems for the men who were trying to settle Indian affairs. The quandary was this: The United States government couldn't solve its Indian problems without land on which to settle the tribes, but the state of Texas retained title to all its own public lands, and Texas wasn't selling. At this point a true friend of the Indian stepped forward.

Robert Simpson Neighbors came to Texas in 1836 when he was twenty years old. He served as quartermaster to the Texas Army, as a member of Jack Hays's Ranging Company, and was a prisoner of Mexico from 1842–1844 after being captured by General Woll during the second taking of San Antonio. In 1845 he was appointed agent to the Lipan Apache and Tonkawa Indians by the Republic of Texas, and when Texas became a state he was reappointed to his post by the United States Government and given the added responsibility of the Comanches. He lost this job in 1849 when the administration in Washington changed, and he filled the interim with a stint in the state legislature where he sponsored a bill creating Indian reservations in Texas. The only such reservation to last is the one assigned to the Alabama and Coushatta tribes near Woodville. It was established in 1854 largely through Neighbors's efforts. In 1853, following the election of Franklin Pierce as president, Neighbors was appointed a supervising agent of the U.S. Indian Service. In 1854, Neighbors and Randolph B. Marcy of the U.S. Army surveyed land on the upper Brazos and the Clear Fork of the Brazos River, laying out two parcels to be set aside for use by Texas Indians. The Penateka Comanches moved onto the 18,576 acre Clear Fork Reservation. Members of the destitute Delaware, Shawnee, Tonkawa, Wichita, and Caddo tribes took up residence on the 38,152 acre Brazos Reservation.

Situated as they were on the boundary between the settlements to the east and the range of the Comanches to the west, these reservations were doomed from the start. On the Comanche reserve, the temptation to join their brothers on the open prairie was ever present and proved to be too much for most of the young men and for many of the older ones who had fond memories of their freewheeling youth. Meanwhile, the white man pushed ever westward, feeling that the land given to the Indian would be put to better use by him. In spite of protection from federal troops at Camp Cooper and Fort Belknap, and in spite of the valiant efforts of Neighbors, white settlers trespassed on the reservations in ever increasing numbers, inviting retaliatory raids by the Indians.

Finally, in 1859, the situation became so untenable that Neighbors had to admit defeat. With an escort of troops, he moved his Indian charges north across the Red River to the Indian Territory. Two weeks after leaving his Indian friends in the Territory, this good and decent man lay dying from a shotgun blast in the dusty street of the village of Belknap. He was the victim of a white man who disagreed with his views on Indians and whom he most likely didn't even know. Though his mission ended in failure, Robert Neighbors left a legacy of direct dealing with the American Indians. His custom of going out into the field instead of sitting at a desk gained the confidence of the Indians and made him, for a time, the most influential white man among the Indians in Texas.

The Civil War brought a respite for the Plains Indians. Neither the North nor the South wanted the Comanches or Kiowas involved in their battles. So the Indians were left alone to regroup and rejuvenate. It is surmised that sometime in the fall of 1863 a pact was made between the remaining tribes on the southern Great Plains. Participants included the Comanches, Kiowas, Kiowa-Apaches, and Southern Cheyennes, along with some Arapahoes and Dakotas. The frequency of Indian raids in Texas and all along the eastern edge of the Great Plains picked up noticeably in 1864 and continued through the first nine months of the following year. By the fall of 1865, however, the tribes again were seeking peace, and through a succession of negotiations and treaty signings, one by one the bands moved onto land set aside for them in the southwestern Indian Territory. The treaties called for, besides the reservation lands, hunting ranges in the Texas Panhandle and the Llano Estacado. The tribes were also entitled to a monthly food ration which included beef.

Between the years 1872 and 1874, millions of buffalo were killed on the high plains. Most were slaughtered by hide hunters, who might kill as many as one hundred animals in a day, the numbers being dictated by how hot the barrels of their big .50 caliber rifles became and how effectively they could shoot before the herd stampeded. Alarmed at the disappearance of their food supply and suffering real deprivation during the winter of 1874 when the promised beef issue didn't always get to them, the Indians grew restive. From this agitated atmosphere emerged a young Comanche shaman named Isatai. He rallied the tribes for one last try at driving the white men off the plains. At sunrise on June 27, 1874, perhaps as many as 700 Comanches, Kiowas, and Southern Cheyennes, led by Quanah Parker, attacked twenty-eight hide hunters camped at Adobe Walls high in the Texas Panhandle. Isatai, the instigator of it all because he had a promise of victory from the Great Spirit, was wrong. At least thirteen Indians were killed, one by Billy Dixon's spectacular "mile long shot" that hit an Indian seated on a horse almost a mile from where Dixon stood. After the shot, the awestruck Indians called off the engagement and faded into the grassy sea.

Before the month of July was over, United States troops were converging on the plains from five directions. In August 1874, General Nelson Miles led a column that destroyed a camp of some 500 warriors on the northeast rim of Palo Duro Canyon. On September 28, 1874, Colonel Ranald Mackenzie surprised remnants of the Kiowas and Comanches in Palo Duro Canyon, set them to rout, burned their camp equipage and belongings, and shot or captured their horses.

Left on the plains with nothing but what they had on their backs they could choose between walking back to the reservation or dying where they were.

Save for an occasional outbreak over the next ten years, the Comanches and their cohorts were gone from the high plains of Texas forever.

Not so the Apaches. Split into two camps by the Comanche incursion into Texas in the early eighteenth century, the Mescaleros—brothers to the Lipans— kept up a constant series of clandestine raids from their reservation in New Mexico. In 1879 a group of them bolted the reservation and linked up with Warm Springs Apaches under Victorio, an acknowledged master of guerilla warfare. They crossed the Rio Grande three times in the winter of 1879–1880 in the Big Bend area, raiding and plundering settlements, isolated ranches, stagecoaches, and wagon trains. The Mescaleros made two attempts to return to their reservation but were stopped both times by federal troops, once at Quitman Canyon and once at Rattlesnake Springs, both sites located near El Paso.

The Mescaleros then returned with Victorio to his camp in the Candelaria Mountains of Mexico. On October 14, 1880, Victorio was killed by a sharpshooter's bullet during a fight with Mexican volunteers at Tres Castillos. In January, 1881, the remaining members of his band attacked a stagecoach in Quitman Canyon. Texas Rangers, in hot pursuit of the raiders, killed eight Apaches and scattered the rest. It was the last Indian fight in Texas.

The ultimate fate of the American Indians in Texas—and elsewhere—was predictable. Their cultures crashed head-on into an empire fueled by the industrial revolution—and they did not survive. Oddly enough, the weaker tribes faired comparatively better than the more powerful ones when they came up against the invading Spaniards and Anglo-Americans. They did not have happiness and good fortune forever but they were, for the most part, not systematically and brutally destroyed. The price of fierce resistance born of power and arrogance proved—as it often has throughout human history—to be a high one indeed.

Perhaps most Indian-white troubles could not have been avoided even if each side had understood the values and ways of the other. But Indians and white settlers rarely understood the other's concepts of land use and ownership, religion, and other significant matters. The white man was revolted by the Indian's brutality in warfare, without ever undertanding its basis in the Indian's deep rooted belief n the spirit world and life after death. The Plains Indians never understood that the settlers of the United States and New Mexico and Texas were essentially one people. They would agree with the United States not to raid in Oklahoma or Kansas or Nebraska, but regarded Texas as a different place, reserved for their own private plundering. Similarly, they saw New Mexican settlers as a different people from Texan settlers. It was a common practice for the Comanches to raid through Texas, bringing horses, captives and other booty to the Comancheros in New Mexico where they would celebrate and trade for goods so they could go back and raid Texas again.

Firmly convinced of the rightness of their positions, the Indians and the

Texan settlers were intractable enemies, neither side giving an inch until the sheer weight of the white man's numbers finally drove the last Indians across the Red River. Oklahoma is now the beneficiary of the rich cultural heritage of those diverse and ancient peoples, and Texas is the home of their red ghosts.

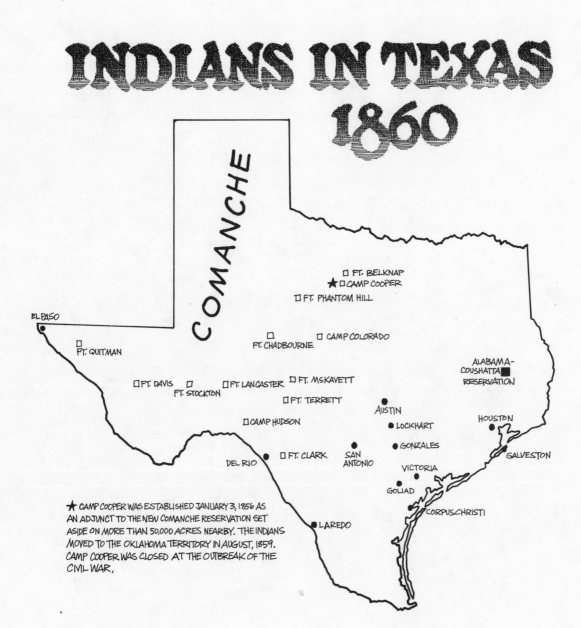

INDIANS IN TEXAS
1860

COMANCHE

EL PASO
☐ FT. QUITMAN

☐ FT. BELKNAP
★ ☐ CAMP COOPER
☐ FT. PHANTOM HILL

☐
FT. CHADBOURNE   ☐ CAMP COLORADO

ALABAMA-
COUSHATTA ■
RESERVATION

☐ FT. DAVIS   ☐   ☐ FT. LANCASTER   ☐ FT. McKAVETT
          FT. STOCKTON

☐ FT. TERRETT
                              AUSTIN
                                              HOUSTON
☐ CAMP HUDSON   ● LOCKHART

                                    ● GONZALES
                        SAN
            ☐ FT. CLARK ANTONIO   GALVESTON
DEL RIO ●   VICTORIA ●

                              GOLIAD ●

★ CAMP COOPER WAS ESTABLISHED JANUARY 3, 1856 AS   CORPUS CHRISTI
AN ADJUNCT TO THE NEW COMANCHE RESERVATION SET
ASIDE ON MORE THAN 50,000 ACRES NEARBY. THE INDIANS
MOVED TO THE OKLAHOMA TERRITORY IN AUGUST, 1859.   ● LAREDO
CAMP COOPER WAS CLOSED AT THE OUTBREAK OF THE
CIVIL WAR.

THEIR ANCESTRAL HOME IS IN THE NORTHEASTERN CORNER OF THE UNITED STATES.

THEIR FIRST CONTACT WITH EUROPEANS HAPPENED WHEN HENRY HUDSON SAILED HIS SHIP THE HALF MOON THROUGH THE ESTUARY AND INTO THE RIVER THAT NOW BEARS HIS NAME.

IT WAS 1660 WHEN THE GREAT MIGRATION OF THE

DELAWARE

BEGAN. PUSHED WESTWARD BY THE ANGLO INVADERS WHO "BOUGHT" THEIR LAND AND BY THEIR POWERFUL ENEMIES THE IROQUOIS, THE TRIBE HAS HISTORICALLY TRIED TO ALIGN ITSELF WITH THE GROWING NUMBERS OF WHITE MEN. THE QUEST FOR FUR, FOR WHICH THE WHITES HAD AN ASTONISHING APPETITE, TOOK THEM ACROSS THE MISSISSIPPI IN 1789 AND THEN, WITH SPANISH BLESSING, INTO KANSAS BY 1800.

JOINED BY OTHER NORTHERN TRIBES IN A SIMILAR PREDICAMENT, THE DELAWARE CROSSED THE RED RIVER INTO TEXAS BETWEEN 1815 AND 1820.

WHILE SMALL BANDS SCATTERED THROUGHOUT THE STATE LOOKING FOR HUNTING GROUNDS THAT WOULD PROVIDE A LIVING, THE MAIN BODY REMAINED IN THE AREA OF THE CADDOS, WHO THE DELAWARES FOUND TO BE THEIR SPIRITUAL BROTHERS. WITH THE ORIGINAL CADDO FARMERS AND THE NEW ONES MOVING IN — CREEK, SHAWNEE, CHICKASAW, CHOCTAW AND CHEROKEE — THE TRIBE THOUGHT THAT THEY HAD, AT LAST, FOUND A HOMELAND.

THEY ADOPTED THE WHITE MAN'S CLOTHING EARLY ON, THINKING THAT THEY MIGHT GET ALONG BETTER WITH THE NEW COMERS IF THEY LOOKED MORE LIKE THEM.

LIKE THEIR NEW ALLIES FROM THE SOUTH-EAST, THEY WERE QUICK TO REALIZE THAT THE THINGS THEY NEEDED TO SURVIVE THE NEW ORDER WERE SCHOOLS, TEACHERS AND TITLE—AS THE SPANISH CALLED IT—TO THE LAND THEY CLAIMED AS THEIR OWN.

BY 1828, THEY HAD MADE NACOGDOCHES THEIR TRADING CENTER AND FAMILIES OF DELA-WARE AND OTHER IMMIGRANT TRIBES WERE A COMMON SIGHT ON THE DUSTY STREETS.

TEXAS' INDEPENDENCE FROM
MEXICO IN 1836 DID NOT BODE WELL
FOR ANY INDIAN IN TEXAS. JUST
AS THE TRIBES IN NORTHEAST
TEXAS HAD BEEN MAKING HEADWAY
WITH THE SPANISH AND THE THE
MEXICANS IN GAINING LEGITIMACY
AS CITIZENS, THE RUSH OF NEW
SETTLERS FROM THE UNITED
STATES TURNED THEIR WORLD
UPSIDE DOWN.

IN SPITE OF THE SYMPATHETIC
VIEWS OF SAM HOUSTON, OTHERS
IN THE TEXAS LEADERSHIP WANTED
THE INDIANS OUT OF THE STATE.
TO ACCOMPLISH THAT GOAL THE
WHITE MEN, IN THEIR COURTS OF
LAW, AWARDED TITLE TO DISPUTED
GROUND, TIME AND AGAIN, TO
OTHER WHITE MEN.

FINALLY, IN 1839, A TRUMPED-
UP CHARGE THAT THE INDIANS IN
NORTHEAST TEXAS HAD HELPED
MEXICO DURING THE REVOLUTION
LEAD TO OPEN WARFARE AGAINST
THE DELAWARE'S FRIENDS THE
CHEROKEES.

ON JULY 15 AND 16 OF 1839, TWO PITCHED BATTLES WERE FOUGHT BETWEEN THE CHEROKEES AND A FEW DELAWARES ON ONE SIDE AND TEXAS TROOPS ON THE OTHER. IN THE END, GALLANT OLD CHIEF BOWLES, FOREVER A FRIEND TO THE WHITE MAN IN SPITE OF ALL THAT THE WHITE MAN DID TO DESTROY THAT FRIENDSHIP, LAY DEAD IN THE EAST TEXAS MUD.
HE WAS WEARING THE SASH AND SWORD GIVEN TO HIM BY SAM HOUSTON.

THE VANQUISHED INDIANS WERE UNCEREMONIOUSLY ROUNDED UP AND DRIVEN NORTH OF THE RED RIVER. THEIR FARMS — SOME OF WHICH HAD BEEN CLEARED AND WORKED FOR AS LONG AS TWENTY YEARS — WERE SOLD AT AUCTION OR SIMPLY TAKEN OVER BY WHITE MEN.

MANY OF THE DELAWARES RAN. THEY JOINED AN ENCLAVE OF THEIR BROTHERS AROUND THE HEADWATERS OF THE PEDERNALES WHERE THEY CONTINUED THEIR FRIENDLY RELATIONSHIP WITH THEIR FEW WHITE NEIGHBORS. IN THIS PART OF THE COUNTRY, THEY NEEDED TO SUPPORT EACH OTHER AGAINST THEIR COMMON ENEMIES — THE APACHES AND COMANCHES.

IN A CONSTANT STATE OF WAR AND EVER ON THE ALERT, THEY HAD MORE AND MORE TROUBLE TURNING THE THIN HILL COUNTRY LAND INTO PRODUCTIVE FARMS. IN 1854, WHEN THE BRAZOS RESERVE WAS SET ASIDE FOR THE INDIANS, MANY OF THE DESTITUTE DELAWARE JOINED EQUALLY POOR AND BELEAGUERED SHAWNEES, TONKAWAS, WICHITAS AND CADDOS ON THE NEW LAND.

THEY NEVER GOT A CHANCE TO MAKE ANYTHING OF THE RESERVATION. IN SPITE OF THE EFFORTS OF INDIAN AGENT ROBERT NEIGHBORS AND THE UNITED STATES ARMY, INCREASING PRESSURE FROM ANGLO SETTLERS FORCED THEM TO MOVE ONCE AGAIN, THIS TIME TO THE INDIAN TERRITORY, WHERE AT LAST THE LONG JOURNEY OF THE DELAWARE CAME TO AN END.

THE SHABBY TREATMENT OF
THE DELAWARE WAS ANSWERED,
FOR THE MOST PART, WITH
KINDNESS. THEY, AND OTHER
INDIAN TRIBES OF THE EARLY
1800s, TRIED AGAIN AND
AGAIN TO MAKE FRIENDS
OF THE VERY PEOPLE WHO
TOOK THEIR LAND, GAVE THEM
ONE DEADLY SICKNESS AFTER
ANOTHER AND, SOMETIMES,
SHOT THEM ON SIGHT.
UNDAUNTED, THE NATIVE
AMERICANS CONTINUED TO
TRY TO FIND A WAY TO
COEXIST.

THEY BECAME FAMOUS
AS SCOUTS—ALONG WITH THE
TONKAWAS AND LIPAN
APACHES—WORKING TIRE-
LESSLY WITH THE RANGERS
AND THE ARMY IN THEIR
EFFORTS TO PROTECT
SETTLERS FROM MARAUDING
HOSTILES.

SADLY, THEIR FAITH IN
THE WHITE MAN WAS ILL-
FOUNDED. ONCE THE THREAT
FROM THE HIGH PLAINS WAS
GONE, THE DELAWARE AND
THEIR FELLOW SCOUTS WERE
EXILED TO THE INDIAN
TERRITORY WITH THE REST
OF THEIR TRIBES.

IN THE BEGINNING THEY WERE SHOSHONI, OR SNAKE, INDIANS, LIVING IN WRETCHED POVERTY ON THE PACIFIC SLOPE OF THE ROCKY MOUNTAINS. BESEIGED BY POWERFUL BLACKFOOT AND CAYUSE NEIGHBORS, ONE SMALL BAND CAUGHT UP NEWLY ARRIVED HORSES AND LEARNED TO RIDE. THEY LEFT THEIR COUSINS AND TOOK TO THE GREAT PLAINS LIKE A TORNADO, BECOMING, IN THE WORDS OF U.S. ARMY GENERAL PHILLIP SHERIDAN, "THE GREATEST LIGHT CAVALRY THE WORLD HAS EVER KNOWN". THEIR WARRIORS BECAME GREAT TRAVELERS, THEIR ORAL HISTORIES LACED WITH TALES OF "ICE MOUNTAINS" (GLACIERS) AND "HAIRY LITTLE MEN WHO LIVE IN THE TREES".

ALTHOUGH THEY DIDN'T REACH TEXAS UNTIL AFTER 1700, AND WERE BANISHED TO THE RESERVATION BEFORE 1890, THEY ARE MOST OFTEN THOUGHT OF WHEN PEOPLE TALK ABOUT TEXAS INDIANS. THEIR ONLY ALLIES WERE THE KIOWAS AND THEY KEPT AN UNEASY PEACE WITH NEW MEXICAN COMANCHEROS WITH WHOM THEY TRADED LIVESTOCK AND SOMETIMES HUMANS STOLEN IN TEXAS AND MEXICO FOR GUNS, AMMUNITION AND OTHER GOODS.

THEY WERE AT WAR WITH EVERYONE ELSE. AT FIRST HONORABLY AND ALMOST JOYOUSLY; AT THE END VICIOUSLY AND BITTERLY. IN THE SIGN LANGUAGE OF THE PLAINS THEIRS WAS THE SNAKE. TEXANS AND MEXICANS AND THE REST OF THE WORLD CALLED THEM

COMANCHES!

SUMMER, 1871. ANGLOS FROM THE UNITED STATES HAVE FLOODED INTO TEXAS. THIRTY-FIVE YEARS EARLIER, SANTA ANNA WAS DEFEATED AT SAN JACINTO. ON DECEMBER 29, 1845, TEXAS BECAME THE 28TH UNITED STATE. THE MEXICAN-AMERICAN WAR HAS BEEN FOUGHT AND WON. CIVIL WAR HAS TORN THE NATION APART AND RECONSTRUCTION IS UNDERWAY. THE FRONTIER IS PATROLLED BY U.S. ARMY TROOPS, SUPPLEMENTED AND OFTEN OVERSHA-DOWED BY QUICK STRIKING TEXAS RANGERS. FEDERAL FORTS STRETCH FROM THE BIG BEND NORTH TO NEAR FT. WORTH — DRAWING A THIN LINE OF DEFENSE BETWEEN NEW SETTLEMENTS IN THE EAST AND THE WESTERN WILDERNESS.

OF THE MORE THAN A DOZEN SEPERATE BANDS OF COMANCHES THAT ONCE ROAMED FREE, THERE REMAIN ONLY THE LARGEST — THE PENETEKA (HONEY EATERS) — THE WILD AND VIOLENT QUAHADI (ANTELOPE), AND WIDELY SCATTERED, VIRTUALLY POWERLESS REMNANTS OF THE OTHERS.

A GROUP OF QUAHADI COMANCHES MOVE SOUTH AND EAST ACROSS THE EDWARDS PLATEAU. TONIGHT, THEY'LL RAISE THEIR SIX TEPEES IN THE CANYONS OF THE UPPER GUADALUPE RIVER. TOMORROW, THE EIGHT WARRIORS WILL CALL ON THEIR PERSONAL "MEDICINE", MOUNT THEIR FASTEST PONIES AND RIDE EAST IN SEARCH OF PLUNDER AND GLORY AROUND THE FAST GROWING SETTLEMENTS.

THEY'LL LEAVE BEHIND THREE OLD MEN AS CAMP GUARDS, ELEVEN GROWN WOMEN, NINE CHILDREN AND TWO MEXICAN SLAVE GIRLS.

THEY'LL TAKE WITH THEM TWO TEEN AGED BOYS, APPRENTICES TO THE FINE ART OF RAIDING. THE BOYS ARE ALONG TO LEARN SKILLS THEY'LL NEVER USE, FOR IN LESS THAN FOUR YEARS, IN 1875, THE QUAHADI CHIEF QUANAH PARKER WILL LEAD THE LAST OF THE WORLD'S WILD COMANCHES, BEATEN, HUNGRY, AND AFOOT, ONTO THE GOVERNMENT RESERVATION AT FT. SILL, OKLAHOMA.

THE RAIDERS TRAVEL UNTIL MIDAFTERNOON, KEEPING TO THE SCATTERED TIMBER AND GULLIES. AFTER PASSING THE GERMAN HILL COUNTRY SETTLEMENT OF FREDRICKSBURG, WITH WHOM THE COMANCHE HAS A LONG-STANDING PEACE TREATY, THEY MAKE A COLD CAMP AND SLEEP UNTIL MIDNIGHT.
FROM NOW ON THEY WILL MOVE ONLY AT NIGHT, BY THE LIGHT OF A COMANCHE MOON.

THE PREY. READING THE MEMOIRS OF THE EARLY PIONEERS IN TEXAS, IT IS OF NOTE THAT THE MAJORITY OF THEM HAD AN ATTITUDE THAT COULD ONLY BE CALLED CAVALIER TOWARDS THE CLEAR AND PRESENT DANGER FROM HOSTILE INDIANS. THAT VERY SENTIMENT WILL PROVE TO BE THIS FAMILY'S UNDOING.

FAR UPRIVER, THE QUAHADI WOMEN SPEND THEIR TIME MAKING THE THINGS THEIR FAMILIES ALWAYS SEEM TO NEED; MOCCASINS, LEGGINGS, PARFLECHES FOR FOOD STORAGE. THEY HAVE MEXICAN SLAVE GIRLS TO DO THE HEAVY CAMP WORK, SUPERVISED BY SHARP-TONGUED GRANDMOTHERS. THE GRANDFATHERS KEEP AN OLD WARRIOR'S WARY EYE WHILE MAKING BOWS AND ARROWS FOR SMALL HANDS AND FLUTES FOR SMALL FINGERS. WHEN LIFE GETS TOO HECTIC, THEY TELL THE OLD STORIES OVER A PIPE OF TOBACCO.

ANGLOS HAVE SETTLED ALONG THE RIVERS, SO THE COMANCHES STICK TO THE RIDGES AND PRAIRIES BETWEEN THE MAJOR DRAINAGES. RESTING BY DAY, HIDDEN IN THE OAK MOTTS AND THICKETS, THEY PENETRATE DEEP INTO THE SETTLEMENTS AND, UNDETECTED, ADD SEVEN HORSES AND A FINE RED MULE TO THEIR WORLDLY POSSESSIONS.

DETOURING AROUND THE GROWING HAMLETS OF NEW BRAUNFELS AND SEGUIN, THEY EMPTY SELECTED CORRALS OF THE BEST LIVESTOCK. THE TWO BOYS LEARN THE MOST SECRET OF TRICKS HERE; HOW TO RELIEVE A SLUMBERING HOMESTEADER OF HIS BEST HORSE WHILE IT'S TIED UP ONLY THIRTY FEET FROM HIS BED.

THEIR BOLDNESS GROWING WITH THEIR CON- TINUING SUCCESS, A DAYBREAK ATTACK ON AN ISOLATED COW CAMP NETS THEM A BRIEF SKIRMISH, BUT TWO POORLY ARMED MEXICANS ARE NO CONTEST AND THEIR SCALPS GO WITH THE FIVE PONIES, THE SUGAR AND THE COFFEE WHEN THE RAIDERS TAKE THEIR LEAVE.

BRAZENLY, THEY TRAIL THEIR HERD ACROSS THE ROLLING COUNTRY AT THE RIM OF THE COASTAL PLAIN AND WHEN THEY SPY A LONE RIDER IN THE DISTANCE THEY MAKE NO ATTEMPT AT CONCEALMENT. INSTEAD, THEY ASSIGN THE YOUNGSTERS TO HOLD THE FIFTY-ODD ANIMALS AND RIDING TOWARD THE UNSUSPECTING QUARRY, LET HIM MAKE THE FIRST MOVE BEFORE BREAKING INTO A FULL GALLOP.

THE SETTLER, CONCERNED OVER THE ABSENCE OF A PREGNANT COW AND DETERMINED TO FIND HER, INSTANTLY FORGETS HIS ERRAND AND WHEELING FOR HOME NEARLY TWO MILES AWAY, HOPES FERVENTLY THAT HE MADE THE RIGHT CHOICE WHEN HE TRADED AWAY HIS FANCY RIDING HORSE FOR A GOOD, STURDY AND PRACTICAL BEAST TO PULL A PLOW.

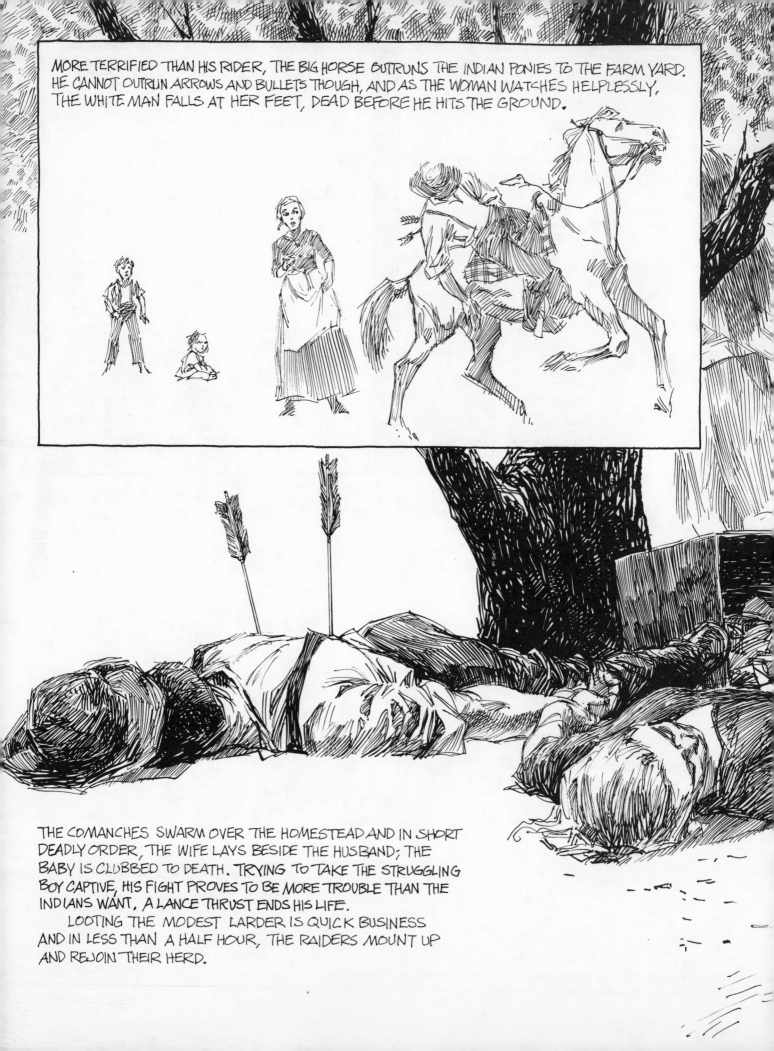

MORE TERRIFIED THAN HIS RIDER, THE BIG HORSE OUTRUNS THE INDIAN PONIES TO THE FARM YARD.
HE CANNOT OUTRUN ARROWS AND BULLETS THOUGH, AND AS THE WOMAN WATCHES HELPLESSLY,
THE WHITE MAN FALLS AT HER FEET, DEAD BEFORE HE HITS THE GROUND.

THE COMANCHES SWARM OVER THE HOMESTEAD AND IN SHORT
DEADLY ORDER, THE WIFE LAYS BESIDE THE HUSBAND; THE
BABY IS CLUBBED TO DEATH. TRYING TO TAKE THE STRUGGLING
BOY CAPTIVE, HIS FIGHT PROVES TO BE MORE TROUBLE THAN THE
INDIANS WANT, A LANCE THRUST ENDS HIS LIFE.
    LOOTING THE MODEST LARDER IS QUICK BUSINESS
AND IN LESS THAN A HALF HOUR, THE RAIDERS MOUNT UP
AND REJOIN THEIR HERD.

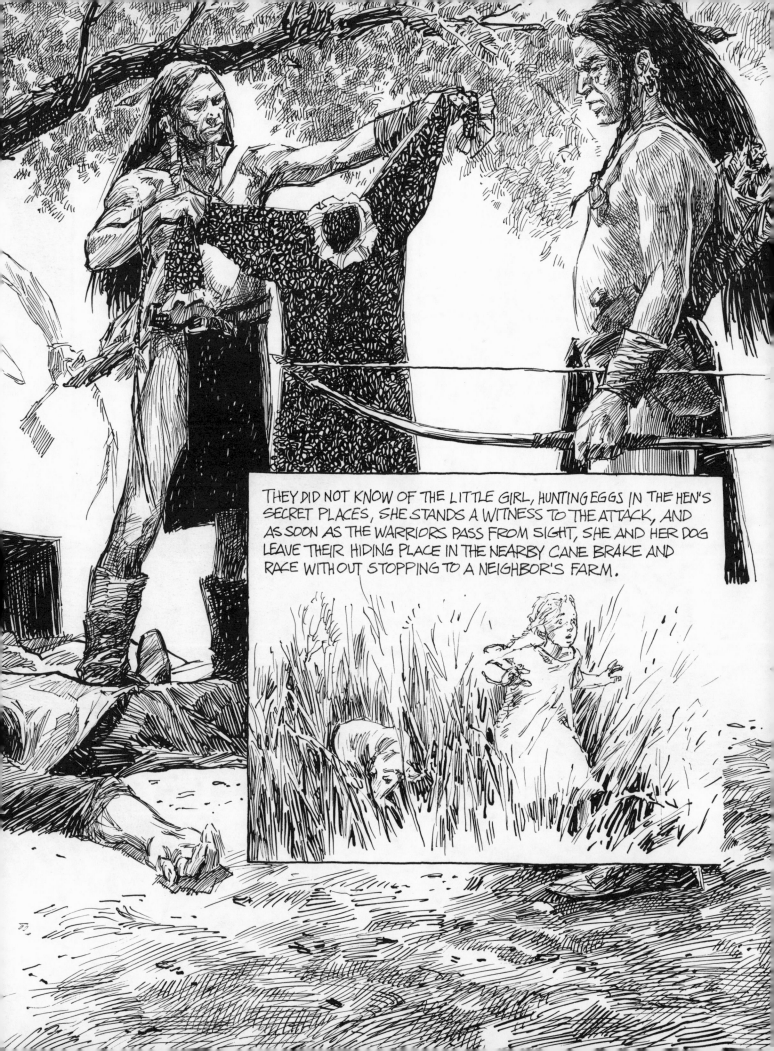

THEY DID NOT KNOW OF THE LITTLE GIRL, HUNTING EGGS IN THE HEN'S SECRET PLACES, SHE STANDS A WITNESS TO THE ATTACK, AND AS SOON AS THE WARRIORS PASS FROM SIGHT, SHE AND HER DOG LEAVE THEIR HIDING PLACE IN THE NEARBY CANE BRAKE AND RACE WITHOUT STOPPING TO A NEIGHBOR'S FARM.

INDIANS ABOUT! THE FIRST ALARM GOES OUT WITH A 12 YEAR OLD BOY ON HORSEBACK. HE RIDES FROM FARM TO FARM AND WHILE THE NEWLY ORPHANED GIRL STILL SOBS, SIX HEAVILY ARMED FARMERS AND THREE TEXAS RANGERS APPEAR.

THE TWO OLDER MEN ARE SENT TO SAN ANTONIO TO ALERT THE MILITARY. THE OTHERS GO TO BURY THE DEAD AND HUNT DOWN THE COMANCHES. WITH 55 HORSES IN THEIR HERD NOW, THEIR TRAIL IS NOT HARD TO FOLLOW.

LEAVING THE STRICKEN HOMESTEAD, THE TEXANS HAVE TWO OBJECTIVES. FIRST IN ORDER IS REVENGE, AND THEN THEY WANT TO TAKE BACK THE STOLEN HORSES.

AS THE RAIDERS PUSH TOWARD THEIR CAMP ON THE GUADALUPE, THEY LEAVE THE BOYS TO WATCH THE BACK TRAIL AND BEFORE LONG, THE VENGEFUL SETTLERS ARE DISCOVERED.

NOW SOUTH OF SEGUIN, THE INDIANS KNOW THE HILL COUNTRY IS WITHIN REACH. PUSHING THE JADED ANIMALS HARD, THEY WANT TO BE IN THAT BROKEN TERRAIN WHERE THEY CAN LOSE THEIR TRAILERS OR FIGHT THEM FROM GOOD COVER.

NIGHT FINDS THEM HIGH ON THE BLANCO, WHERE THEY STOP TO REST THE WORN OUT ANIMALS. THEY HAVE COME A LONG WAY AND GONE TO MUCH TROUBLE TO STEAL THESE HORSES AND THEY'LL NOT RUN THEM TO DEATH.

WHEN THE MEXICANS AND WHITES WERE ONLY A FEW, THE RAIDING WAS A GAME PLAYED FOR HONOR AND GLORY AMONG PEERS. NOW THOUGH, THE INVADERS ARE SO MANY THAT THE TWO WARRIORS WHO WATCH THE TEXAN'S CAMP SENSE THE CHANGE. THEY KNOW THAT THEIR WAY OF LIFE IS IN REAL PERIL — THEIR ONLY OPTIONS REMAINING ARE TO FIGHT OR TO SUBMIT TO THE WHITE MAN'S WAYS. COMANCHES DO NOT SUBMIT.

BEFORE FIRST LIGHT THE COMANCHES ARE MOVING. ONE OF THE BOYS IS SENT AHEAD, FOR THE GRANDFATHERS MUST MOVE THE CAMP BEFORE UNWELCOME COMPANY ARRIVES.

BEFORE THE TEXANS STIR, THE SCOUTS HAVE ALREADY MOVED A MILE UP THE TRAIL AND FINDING A LIKELY SPOT, THEY WAIT IN AMBUSH.

THEY LET THE FIRST WHITE MAN PASS AND LOOSE A FLIGHT OF ARROWS INTO THE REST OF THE GROUP. LEAPING ASTRIDE THEIR HORSES, THE WARRIORS BEGIN THE RUNNING BATTLE. WITHOUT THE TEXANS REALIZING IT, THEY ARE LURED FAR TO THE NORTH AND EAST, AWAY FROM THE PATH OF THE MAIN BODY OF COMANCHES.

THE CHASE SERPENTINES THROUGH THE CANYONS AND OVER THE HIGH MEADOWS. DODGING AND WEAVING EXPERTLY, THE INDIANS NEVER ALLOW THE TEXANS A CLEAN SHOT. THEY DO NOT STAND AND FIGHT FOR GOOD REASON; THEIR QUIVERS ARE NEARLY EMPTY OF ARROWS AND THEY HAVE ONLY 4 ROUNDS IN THE ONLY PISTOL THEY CARRY.

IT IS ALMOST NOON WHEN A RANGER FINALLY BRINGS DOWN ONE HORSE. IN FALLING HE PINS HIS RIDER TO THE GROUND AND THE RAIDER IS SHOT BEFORE HE CAN FIT AN ARROW TO HIS BOW.
HIS COMRADE, WHO STOPPED TO HELP HIM, PULLS THE TRIGGER ON AN EMPTY CHAMBER AND DIES AT THE SIDE OF HIS FRIEND.

NOT KNOWING THE COUNTRY AND FAR OFF THE STOLEN HORSES' TRAIL, THE TEXANS MUST CONTENT THEMSELVES WITH THIS SMALL MEASURE OF REVENGE. THE LOSS OF TWO WARRIORS IS NO SMALL MEASURE FOR THE QUAHADI, AND THE WAILING OF THE WOMEN ATTESTS TO THE FEARFULLY HIGH PRICE OF HORSEFLESH.

BOOK FOUR . . . TWENTIETH CENTURY

*"They made us promises, more than I can remem-
ber, but they never kept but one. They promised to
take our land and they took it."*

from *North American Indian*,
by Christopher Davis

Now, in the last half of the 1980s, there are about 65,000 American Indians living in Texas. They represent over 190 different tribes from Comanche to Iroquois, Apache to Crow, Seminole to Inuit. They are here for jobs and careers, doing everything from construction labor to farm and ranch work, and from owning automobile dealerships to managing multi-million dollar companies and federal and state agencies. Just over 1,800 Indians live on the three reservations in the state, but the vast majority of the Native Americans are found among the rest of us, living as the rest of us do.

Of the reservations in Texas, the Tigua in El Paso, the Kickapoo in Eagle Pass and the Alabama-Coushatta between Livingston and Woodville, none is populated by Indians who lived here when the Spaniards arrived. To visit the Caddos or the descendants of the Tonkawas you will need to travel to Oklahoma. The Comanches and Wichitas can be found there also. The Coahuiltecan, Ataka-pan, Karankawa, and Jumano are gone. In the early part of the 1970s, only a handful of Lipan Apaches of pure blood remained at the Mescalero Reservation near Riudoso, New Mexico.

The Jumanos, first imposed upon by the Spaniards at El Paso del Norte, were the first to move out. While some were reduced to slavery by the Europeans, another group is known to have moved out onto the Southern Plains where they became buffalo hunters, forsaking their traditional way of life as a fair trade for freedom. It is suspected that this group of Jumanos merged with the Apaches early on, about 1650–1670.

A few years later, up the Rio Grande at Santa Fe, a revolution was brewing in the pueblos. Having had their fill of the duplicity and oppression of the Spanish interlopers and finding themselves caught in the middle of a power struggle between the church and the civil authorities, the normally peaceful farmers of northern New Mexico armed themselves. On August 20, 1680, they laid seige to the town of Santa Fe—"spreading destruction among the houses of the district and setting fire to the hermitage of San Miguel." So ferocious was the attack that those Spaniards who could do so retreated down the Rio Grande all the way to El Paso del Norte (present-day Juarez), seeking protection from the soldiers at the presidio there. They took with them 317 Tigua Indians (Tigua is the Spanish phonetic spelling of Tiwa, one of the Pueblo Indian languages), who were either converted Mission Indian refugees or natives impressed to carry the baggage; the record is not clear on their status. A second group of 385 Isleta Tiguas was moved shortly thereafter, this time decidedly against their will, in an effort to keep them from joining the revolt. A number of the Tiguas escaped the Spanish round-up and hid among the Hopi and other pueblo people nearby. When the dust had settled, they came out of hiding and rebuilt the Isleta Pueblo in New Mexico at its original site thirteen miles south of Albuquerque. The Tiguas who were moved to the south have the dubious distinction of being, possibly, the first Native Americans relocated to accommodate the Europeans. They stopped on the north shore of the Rio Grande, which was at flood stage, and named their new home Ysleta del Sur or, Isleta of the South.

Thus separated from their relatives in the north, the Tiguas were forced by the missionaries to build the Ysleta Mission that stands today. The foundation and major portions of the adobe walls in the current structure were built by Tigua hands two hundred years ago. The church has been in continuous use since 1682 and, though it has suffered heavy damage from fire and an assortment of other disasters through the years, it is still the church of St. Anthony to the Tigua. The Feast of St. Anthony, on June 13th, is their principal religious celebration.

The Tiguas practiced then, and still practice now, a curious blend of Roman Catholicism and their traditional religion. They have managed to combine and mold the two into one that they can live with, adjusting their own feast days to coincide with church celebration days and managing, in that fashion, to get along quite well with the Spanish and Mexican clergy and civilian authorities. They even served as scouts for military campaigns in West Texas and the border areas.

They would probably have continued in this manner to the present day had it not been for the 1848 Treaty of Guadalupe Hidalgo which, though it guaranteed them United States citizenship and—at least in writing—protected their property, opened the way for an influx of Anglo-Americans into the border region. Spurred on by the discovery of gold in California, white men appeared in increasing numbers, for El Paso lay on a direct route to El Dorado.

Over the next twenty-odd years, while the federal government was handing out land in wholesale lots to the New Mexican pueblos, the Tigua of Ysleta del Sur were ignored. So in 1871, when the Texas legislature passed a law that made the pueblo area a part of the city of Ysleta, giving the city the authority to dispose of land to actual settlers or speculators, the fox was in the hen house. The Tiguas lost virtually all their holdings by deception, by legal maneuverings, or by outright force to predatory white men. The law was stricken from the books as unconstitutional two years later, but the deals had been made, and the Tiguas were the big losers.

For nearly a hundred years, the Tiguas languished near their lost homes. Over a period of time, they built new structures of traditional adobe, and they continued to bake their daily bread in the pueblo style *horno*—the adobe, beehive-shaped outdoor oven. Although people in the area were aware of them, anthropologists and assorted experts periodically published announcements of their final extinction.

They were dramatically discovered once again when, on March 15, 1955, the city of El Paso annexed Ysleta, making the Tiguas subject to property taxes. To avoid foreclosure proceedings, the average Tigua family would have to come up with $100 a year despite having a average family income of under $400 per year.

As their cousins had done in 1680, the Tiguas rose up against oppressors: this time they waged a legal battle which resulted in their official recognition as a legitimate Native American tribal entity, entitled to the protection of the federal and state governments.

The Tigua Indian Reservation today, the Ysleta del Sur Pueblo, is in the historic Mission district about fifteen miles south-southwest of downtown El Paso. The main part of the reservation is 27.8 acres, housing the administrative complex, the arts and crafts center, and a cultural complex. Also on the property is a 113 unit housing community, a multi-purpose community center/recreation area, and a community laundromat.

The Tigua Indian Arts and Crafts Center/Cultural Complex houses a restaurant serving a menu of Indian, Tex-Mex, and basic American food. It features the traditional Tigua red and green chili and prize-winning fajitas. Tourists here are encouraged to visit the Living-Arts Pueblo, a replica of a pueblo community where they can see artisans and craftsmen in different areas making pottery and baking bread. In the Dance Plaza a variety of pueblo social dances are performed on a regular basis. There is also a display of cultural and historic artifacts. Close by, the Candelaria/Alderete house, built about 1800, has been converted into a dinner restaurant while managing to conserve its historical integrity. The Ysleta Mission is next door to the Arts and Crafts Center. All together, Tigua land scattered about El Paso County adds up to about 97 acres.

The Tigua of Ysleta del Sur think that they are due, at the very least, compensation for the four league grants they were denied in 1864 when their cousins in New Mexico received their land. In addition, they claim aboriginal title to much of the El Paso area as being "that area which they controlled by exclusive use and by defending it against intruders and other groups." To the east, the Hueco Mountains and Hueco Tanks State Park have become bones of contention.

The area is revered as the Tigua's traditional hunting grounds, usurped for the white man's use.

Whether or not the land issues are resolved, the timetable for Tigua self-sufficiency is moving along at a brisk pace. They expect that by 1990 their various enterprises on and near the reservation will provide a substantial part of the tribal income while giving jobs to several tribal members. To be sure, all is not completely well at Ysleta del Sur. Major problems still await or elude solutions; but progress from year to year is visible.

Downstream on the Rio Grande near Eagle Pass, the Texas Band of the Kickapoos are just beginning their journey into mainstream America.

The Kickapoos were first encountered by Europeans in the Great Lakes region in 1640. Through a series of treaties and agreements, the tribe was pushed and shoved even farther west and south until they ended up in Illinois, where the band broke into two factions over the suitability of reservation land in Missiouri. One part of the band relocated near Fort Leavenworth, Kansas. The second part fled to the Sabine River in Texas, where they settled in with other tribes recently moved into the area.

When Texas gained its independence from Mexico in 1836, the southern band split again, one part of them going into the Indian Territory north of the Red River. About eighty Kickapoos went south, crossing the Rio Grande and settling near Morelos, Coahuila, about forty miles south of Eagle Pass. A more substantial number of Kickapoo were persuaded to come south to Morelos in 1850 by the Seminole Chief Wild Cat, but two years later, all but about twenty Indians returned to the main body in Oklahoma at the urging of their chiefs.

Ten years later, growing discontent with their treatment on the reservations prompted the migrations to begin anew. In January, 1865, 1,300 men, women, and children left the Indian Territory to rejoin others in Mexico. They rode far to the west of the Texas settlements, giving those dangerous places a wide berth. Nevertheless, they were discovered moving through the country near San Angelo and on the old Fryer Ranch, about sixteen miles south of that city, where Spring and Dove creeks join, they were attacked by 370 state border guards led by Captain Henry Fossett. This was not the first unprovoked attack upon peaceful Indians nor would it be the last; and in this case it was a bad call by the good captain. Rallying around No-Ko-Wat, the Kickapoos recovered from the initial surprise and administered a sound thrashing to the Texans, killing 36 and wounding 60 more before the Anglo-Americans could get away.

The Kickapoos continued on to Mexico and for several years acted as surrogate border guards, fighting off Apaches and Comanches and occasionally raiding Texan settlements. The Mexican government was so thankful for their presence on the river that first Benito Juarez and later Venustiano Carranza saw fit to give them 17,000 acres in the mountains as payment for their service.

Between 1871 and 1873, the United States government, in an effort to stop the Kickapoo raids in Texas, attempted to persuade the Mexican Indians to rejoin

their relatives in Oklahoma. In 1873, while the Bureau of Indian Affairs was negotiating with the Indians, and while the Kickapoo warriors were away from their
families, a U.S. military party stole across the border and kidnapped what women
and children they could find, taking them north to Oklahoma. Later in that year,
300 Kickapoos were persuaded to follow the captives north. In 1875, two more
groups went north, leaving only about 350 Kickapoos in Nacimiento, Coahuila,
here they had settled.

In Oklahoma, nothing seemed to go right. The Kickapoos were thoroughly
displeased with the cavalier manner in which they were handled by the government. There was not enough of anything. Pressure on them increased to put their
children in school and to forsake their traditional way of life. When whites moved
to exploit the land that was ostensibly theirs forever, the Kickapoos had had
enough.

In 1898, two-thirds of the Oklahoma tribe moved back to Mexico. However, they retained close ties with their Oklahoma brethern. Using a "pass" given
them by the United States government in 1832, they moved freely back and forth
across the Mexican-United States border—a line that they never recognized
anyway.

In the 1940s, a severe drought in Mexico dried up their fields and reduced
the game population. To survive, the Kickapoos were forced to find another way to
live, so they became migrant farm workers. Leaving a small number of their own
in Nacimiento, the majority of the tribe moved to a site that they had used for a
hundred years as a campground in their travels. On the north bank of the Rio
Grande at Eagle Pass, it now happened to be under the International Bridge. From
here they moved into the migrant worker stream each April and May, following
the harvest north as far as Montana and the Dakotas. On the way they visited with
their relatives in Oklahoma.

While some of the Kickapoos continued to return to the Mexican moun-
tains every winter—from November to March—many of them settled in at Eagle
Pass. The band's migratory life style didn't fit the mold made by the Bureau of
Indian Affairs who had a Kickapoo Reservation set aside in Oklahoma. So the
Texas Band of the Kickapoos, as they came to be called, remained in limbo—an
American Indian tribe without government recognition. No recognition in this
instance meant that no health, education, or job-training programs were provided
to the tribe, and they were left to sink ever deeper into grinding poverty beneath
the bridge. They were without bona fide citizenship in either country. Mexico said
that it had given them land but they chose to live in the United States. The United
States said that the tribe had a reservation in Oklahoma with government services
provided there. If these Kickapoos wanted to take advantage of those services,
they should go to Oklahoma. In fairness to the bureaucrats, they were theoreti-
cally right. Agreements had been signed and the government, in its way, was holding up its end of the bargain. But the Texas Band had been betrayed too many
times and so they stayed away. To compound the problem, lack of provable citi-

zenship left state and local governments with no other choice but to deny them what public assistance and health services were available.

Beginning in 1971, private individuals and church leaders began a movement to have the Kickapoos in Eagle Pass recognized as a legitimate tribe. It wasn't until September of 1981 that legislation was introduced in the United States Congress granting federal recognition to the Band; and in 1983, the Texas Band of Kickapoo Act was finally signed into law.

The law provided the following: that the Texas Band of the Kickapoos would become fully eligible for all federal services available to other Indians; that the Department of the Interior should take land into trust for the Band in Maverick County, Texas; that all the Band members who wanted United States citizenship and its benefits would be granted the same; that those who chose not to ask for citizenship would be issued passes allowing them to cross the Mexican-United States border at will. These non-citizen Kickapoos would be entitled to the same rights and benefits as citizens of the United States except for the right to vote and to hold public office. Although the law provided for the Bureau of Indian Affairs to hold land in trust for the Texas Band of the Kickapoos, it remained consistent with the government policy of one tribe, one reservation. No taxpayer money was appropriated to buy land for the Kickapoos.

It was left to private initiative to fill this void. Individuals, church groups, and foundations, acting under the umbrella name of the "Kickapoo Land Acquisition Committee," provided the money to purchase 125.4 acres of land eight miles down the Rio Grande from Eagle Pass. The Kickapoos were granted clear title to the land in January, 1985. The same year the legislature of the state of Texas amended the statutes of the Texas Indian Commission—the agency that administers the other two reservations in the state—to include the Texas Band of the Kickapoo Indians. While the federal government holds the land in trust, the state is responsible for assisting the Kickapoos in development of health, educational, agricultural, business, and industrial programs.

Through all their migrations and trials, the Kickapoos have clung fast to their traditional ways. They are a tightly knit group with strong family values and religious beliefs still universally practiced through the band. They are decidedly the most traditional of all the Native American groups in the United States. All of the members speak the native Algonquian dialect. About three-fourths of them speak Spanish as a second language and only about 10–20 percent speak English as a third language.

The Kickapoos will not give up their ancient traditions. The difficult task ahead of them now is to retain their culture while, at the same time, raising their standard of living and moving into the mainstream of twentieth-century American life. They will be helped along this path by the Kickapoo Land Development Committee (the successor to the Kickapoo Land Acquisition Committee), the Indian Health Service, the Bureau of Indian Affairs, the Oklahoma Kickapoo Tribe and the Texas Indian Commission. They are hard at work building the facitilities to house a community center, child care facility, health care services, a community water system, roads, and home sites on their new land.

About 600 people live on the reservation now, though as many as half of them will be gone from May to October, following the crops north. Ten of the Kickapoos have received their high school diplomas, and two ladies have completed secretarial school in Eagle Pass. The tribe will send eighty children to the Eagle Pass Public School System in the fall of 1987. While progress is slow, it is also certain.

As the Kickapoos struggle to their feet on the border and the Tiguas progress well in El Paso, the most well-known Indian Reservation in the state is that of the Alabama-Coushatta, near Livingston in East Texas. The 510 members of the two tribes living on the 4,766-acre reservation in Polk County have made tourism a major business. Upwards of 100,000 visitors a year take advantage of their gift shop, restaurant, and concession stands, the Living Indian Village, the arts and crafts center and museum, the camping and fishing facilities, and several bus and train tours of the Big Thicket. Many tribal members are employed in the tourist business and others find work in the lumber industry close by. Now, natural gas has been discovered beneath the reservation land; the implications of that find do not have to be explained.

The future of the Alabama and the Coushatta was not always so bright. Their traceable history begins when Hernando de Soto recorded that his troops attacked a village of "Alibamy" in what later became northwestern Mississippi. He also reported that they visited a tribe of "Koasati" whose principal village was on an island in the Tennessee River, most likely the one now known as Pine Island.

For 160 years the two tribes were, mercifully, left alone. When next heard from in 1702, the Coushatta were first, combatants, and then allies of the French on the upper Alabama River. They remained the subject of French journals until 1763 when Great Britain took over the American southeast. At that time, a large portion of the Coushatta were living on the Tombigbee River and in 1795, they moved to the Trinity River in Texas.

The history of the Alabama is a bit sketchier. They were reported by the French to be carrying on little battles with the Mobile Indians around Mobile Bay in 1701. When the French built Fort Toulouse near the meeting of the Coosa and Tallapoosa rivers in 1717, peace was established between the two tribes and trade became their major preoccupation.

The French chronicles note that the Alabama lived a relatively sedate life in log houses. The women spent most of their time cultivating small patches of melons, corn, rice, potatoes, and a variety of herbs, while the men hunted. After wandering through several southern states, a segment of the Alabamas moved into what is now Texas in the early 1800s, settling at Peach Tree Village in Tyler County in 1816 with about 1,000 people. The Alabama and Coushatta occupied most of the Big Thicket with settlements in Polk, Tyler, San Jacinto, Trinity and Angelina counties when white settlers began to move into the area in serious numbers. By 1830, more than 10,000 whites were east of the Brazos River with Nacogdoches and San Augustine becoming large and thriving towns. While the tribes carried on extensive trade with the Anglo-Americans, they worked hard at staying separate.

During the Texas war for independence, Mexican agents actively tried to recruit Alabama and Coushatta assistance along with that of other tribes in the area. The Indians refused to be involved, preferring to let the war take its course. When the Texans prevailed, the Indians stepped forward to render what assistance was needed to get the Texans back on their feet. This friendship was not forgotten by Sam Houston, for when other tribes were pushed to the Brazos River reservations in the 1850s and finally exiled to the Indian Territory, the Alabamas and Coushattas were given 1,280 acres of land on Big Sandy Creek, exactly where they wanted to be. Title was given to the Alabamas and the land was given tax free status, forming the core of the present-day reservation. In 1855 the Texas Legislature approved a grant of 640 acres of land for the Coushattas. The land turned out to be unsuitable for crops and too densely wooded for cattle. Though the Indians hunted in the Thicket, that region soon showed signs of overuse and a steady decline in living conditions set in on the reservation.

In 1928, Clem Fain, Jr., an agent for the reservation, took Chief Charles M. Thompson and Sub-Chief McConnico Battise to Washington where they appeared before Congress, the Commissioner of Indian Affairs, and President Calvin Coolidge. Hunger and starvation on the reservation were pervasive. Housing conditions were abysmal. The federal government got the message. It bought 3,071 acres of land next to the original reservation and furnished money for better housing, new wells , and educational and medical needs. The Alabama-Coushatta Reservation was put under Federal Trust from 1928 until 1953 when it was returned to State Trust, one of the few Indian reservations in the United States today that is not under Federal Trust.

Although the reservations serve as a focus for Indian heritage in Texas, with the majority of Native Americans living elsewhere, there is still the difficulty of remaining a traditional Indian, while at the same time pursuing the American Dream. To help bridge the gap, a litany of self-help groups, council, committees and foundations exist for the benefit of the Urban Indian, as native Americans living off the reservation are called. Most of these organizations are centered in Dallas, where the majority of the people they serve live, but others are to be found in Houston, San Antonio and Austin. All have strong ties to the Texas Indian Commission which acts as a liaison between the Indians and the government.

These organizations have found that native Americans in Texas have the same problems as native Americans in the rest of the United States. As a group, Indians have the lowest educational level, highest unemployment, poorest health, worst housing, greatest poverty, and fewest public services of any group or population in the country. They are often the subject of prejudice and discrimination.

In Texas, Indians in El Paso, Houston, and Dallas/Fort Worth have an average of 9.3 years of education compared to 12½ years for others competing for the same jobs. As might be expected, four in ten Indians in Texas are unemployed compared to one in ten workers of other races. The median per capita annual income of Indians in Texas is $2,706 compared to $6,683 for the rest of the state. Half of the Indians in Texas live beneath the poverty level while less than two in ten Texans of other races are as poor. The Kickapoos are much poorer than even other Indians, with seven out of ten living below the poverty level.

As a consequence of their eduational and economic short falls, most Indian housing is substandard. Infant mortality rate for Indians is 18.2 deaths per 1,000 births as opposed to 16.1 per 1,000 births for non-Indians. Only one in three Texas Indians will live long enough to collect social security. Their young people, ages 15 to 24, are killing themselves off at a ghastly pace. Motor vehicle deaths among this age group are four times the national average and the suicide rate three times the national norm. Diabetes, renal failure, tuberculosis, and alcoholism kill Indians at what can only be termed epidemic rates.

For Indians in Texas, it is a long and difficult journey, this entering into the white man's world and competing on an equal footing, while at the same time remaining true to the ancient cultures and customs of their fathers. The avowed goal of the Indians in Texas is to work themselves, or their children, into the position of being free of government aid, at least in the twentieth century context. They now have a structure of support systems and educational opportunities to help them accomplish these economic and spiritual goals. It is the charge now of each generation to see to it that the next generation starts one step farther up the ladder without losing touch with their precious heritage.

Just before this book went to press, President Ronald Reagan signed into law on August 19, 1987 legislation that returned the Alabama-Coushatta and Tigua lands to the federal trust. This action puts the weight of the Federal Government behind the Indians, protecting their lands from encroachment, and opening the door to programs and funds heretofore unavailable to them. The Texas Indian Commission, which worked hard for this action, is justifiably pleased.

INDIANS IN TEXAS
1987

TIGUA RESERVATION–EL PASO

ALABAMA-COUSHATTA
RESERVATION–WOODVILLE

KICKAPOO RESERVATION
EAGLE PASS

PHOTOGRAPHER'S INTRODUCTION

Indians in Texas today are as diverse as any other ethnic group—and not nearly as identifiable. Indians, in fact, generally see themselves not as Indians, but as tribal members. An Indian is Cherokee or Creek, or Tigua or Kickapoo, not "Indian". "Indian" is a term the white man coined to refer to the population of a continent.

In traveling the state to photograph Indians today—what they do and how they are like or unlike any other Texans—I saw a remarkable diversity—from an individual living in extreme poverty on the banks of the Rio Grande to a successful lawyer with a corner office high over Main Street in downtown Dallas. I saw educational diversity—from a college graduate schoolteacher in Weatherford to people in east El Paso who never went to school at all and speak no English. I saw resentment for past sins and anger for present disadvantages. I also saw hope for the future, especially for the youth, and I saw resolve for better living conditions and increased education.

I saw assimilation into the modern American urban culture and economic system, yet a pride in one's ancient Indian culture and tribal identity. But a culture cannot be both maintained and assimilated. I saw pride in language and traditions that are being forgotten. I saw grandparents' pride in their children's education and economic improvement, but sadness that their children were not teaching the native language to the grandchildren.

In my quest I was met sometimes with suspicion—I am a non-Indian—but never with hostility. I was received graciously and with hospitality in private homes and was offered meals and beds to sleep in. The Native Americans I met were generous and honest. I hope the following look at their lives is caring and generous as well.

—Reagan Bradshaw

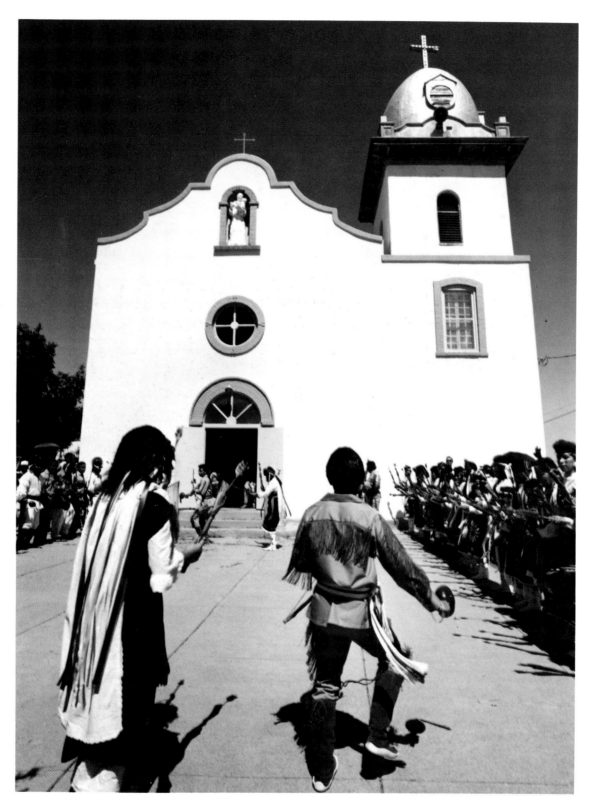

June 13 Saint Anthony's day celebration in front of the church at Ysleta del Sur. After morning mass, symbolic flagellation on the church steps is followed by dances to the Green Corn and then a parade through the streets to the Tigua community a mile away for the traditional feast. On the facing page, some celebrants.

Pistolero Marty Silvas fires shots into the air periodically during the dances to frighten away bad spirits.
Above, a final touch of paint for a Tigua beauty's costume.

Executive Director of the Texas Indian Commission Raymond Apodaca, a Tigua, leads the parade.

Tribal Council Governor Miguel (Mike) Pedraza with the tribe's ceremonial drum and Lawrence Lujan, who studies for a degree in business at the University of Texas at El Paso while working as a cashier and host at the Tigua Indian Restaurant.

Mike Silvas, handyman at the Tigua Indian Arts and Crafts Center. Joe Sierra is manager of special programs at the El Paso Convention and Visitors Bureau and poses here in his ceremonial dress.

Romana Pais

Christina Gutierrez

Hermilla Silvas

*Traditional Kickapoo homes on the newly created Texas Band
of Kickapoo Reservation east of Eagle Pass.*

Nakia Breen, Cherokee, with her adopted Kickapoo son Kikakineta ("captured by another tribe").

Jesusita Gonzalez with children Gary, Crystal and Christine.

Rosalie Gonzalez, Kickapoo from Nacimiento, Mexico.

Michael Suke, Oklahoma Kickapoo-Potowatomi.

Vicente and Cecilia Jalan Lopez. He is a member of the Kickapoo Tribal Council.

David Alcoze, Cherokee, is an art teacher in the Dallas Independent School District and former director of the now defunct DISD Native American Cultural Center.

Cherokee Frank McLemore is a civil servant with the Affirmative Employment Programs Office of the U.S. Office of Personnel Management and deeply involved in the Tribal American Network.

At the top of the facing page Ken Martinez, Laguna Pueblo, is an employment training counselor with the Dallas InterTribal Center in Oak Cliff.

Gregory G. Gomez, Lipan Apache and civil servant with the U.S. Department of Health and Human Services Administration for Children, Youth and Families makes a point at a meeting of the American Indian Advisory Committee to the Dallas Independent School District.

Ken Brown, Sioux and Creek, volunteers stories and demonstrations of Indian culture at the Dallas Public Library where he is also employed as a professional artist. Choctaw Richard Lester poses in front of the Pit Stop USA franchise that he manages in Dallas.

Arnold S. Battise, Alabama-Coushatta, is an attorney with the Office of the General Counsel to the U.S. Department of Health, Education and Welfare in Dallas.

At left, Ken Brown in his story telling dress. Above, Cherokee Frances Campbell-Vereen, education and research consultant in Weatherford.

Pat Peterson, Choctaw, a graduate of SMU with a degree in Sociology and Psychology administers a Senior Citizens Center for Dallas County from her office at Cedar Springs Methodist Church.

Linda St. Amant, Sioux, is an investigator with the Equal Employment Opportunity Commission in Dallas. She is also the outgoing treasurer of the Texas State American Indian Woman's Association, Inc.

Cathy Gomez and son Itsa-lichii (Red Eagle) at home.

Nelson Celestine is manager of the Tribal Tourist Complex at the Alabama-Coushatta Reservation. Some performers at the Tribal Dance Square are pictured on the facing page.

Alabama-Coushatta tribal members work in many trades. Joe John, above, is a contract bricklayer in Livingston. Maurice Bullock is a welder, a former Tribal Council Chairman and coach of the men's fast pitch softball team.

At the top of the next page, Nelson Celestine is a welder when he's not managing the Tribal Tourist Complex. Jerry Thompson is the first Indian to be licensed as a barber in Texas. He's shown here in front of his home purchased through the HUD building program in the 1960s.

Alabama-Coushatta Chief for Life Fulton Battise.

Alabama-Coushatta Reservation cemetary.

AFTERWORD

*"If true, it's interesting.
If untrue, it's interesting anyway."*

—Mark Twain

One of the pitfalls of research for a book like this is that you turn up information that, while interesting, does not fit within the parameters of the discussion. Such is the case of this book. While the history of the Indian in American can be traced with reasonable accuracy from the European landings up to the present, the record of man in the Americas before then has to be based—save for Mesoamerican codexes—on educated guesses made by archaeologists in their examination of artifacts.

It seems that the more answers you find, the more questions you have. Two of these questions seem to have more answers than can be reconciled: Who were the first Europeans in the Americas? And When did man first come to the western hemisphere?

Stories of New World visitors from China, Phoenicia, Greece and Rome and lost Atlantis will not go away. Speculation about Vikings, African Kings and Egyptians appear in the literature with persistence. According to various sources, all of these wayfarers supposedly made contact with the Indians in Texas long before Columbus arrived, to say nothing of Cabeza de Vaca. However, none of them left a mark of their undisputed presence.

The trail that these early travelers apparently favored was up the Rio Grande from the Gulf of Mexico as far as Santa Elena Canyon and sometimes on to northern New Mexico. Evidence of these travels, proponents say, is found among the pictographs on canyon walls following this trail.

There is, for instance, a book called the Shan Hai King, supposedly the world's oldest geography text. It was written in China in 2205 B.C. and describes a journey through country which some historians say could be the western United States, including some areas of the Trans-Pecos region in Texas.

In 1962, two families named Nickles and Uzzell were visiting Indian Hot Springs in the Big Bend. Donald Uzzell climbed the cliffs on the Tornillo Creek side and about thirty feet above the creek bed he found a broken clay tablet tucked away in a small niche. When the clay fragments were reassembled, it was evident that someone had inscribed strange characters on the face of the tablet. Scrambling down the cliff, Uzzell showed the tablet to his companions and Charles Nickles took photographs of these curious markings.

On leaving the park they left the tablet with a park ranger for safe-keeping. The tablet's marking still made them curious, and after showing the photographs around, they learned that the markings were a phonetic language, related to early Greek and written in a blend of Judean Hebrew and Sidonian Phoenician alphabets. This was an odd combination that is commonly found in Europe, but not a mainstay of Texas ground findings such as arrowheads. Could it be that ancient Phoenicians traveled up and then back down the Rio Grande?

The few scholars who think so will probably agree with Gloria Farley who has a collection of rocks that she says shows traces of writing left by Phoenicians or Libyans who visited, or perhaps even settled, in Oklahoma more than two thousand years ago.

Just as unproven as age-old letters from Phoenicians but more widely believed are the stories of St. Brendan. He was an Irish priest, also known as "the Navigator," who bobbed about the Atlantic Ocean in his skin boat around 550 A.D. His voyage was duplicated as nearly as possible by an expedition sponsored by the National Geographic Society some years ago just to prove it could have been done. Though the journal of the priest's travels does not mention an area that can be readily identified as Texas, he does seem to have entered the Gulf of Mexico.

Another collection of stories from the British Isles concern the travels of a Welsh Prince named Madoc ab Owain Gwynedd, who may have landed in the Gulf of Mexico around 1170 A.D. There are also reports of Indians in Alabama who spoke Welsh. The saga and the Indians were proof enough for the Daughters of the American Revolution to place a marker at Mobile Bay commemorating Prince Madoc's landing.

In 1311 A.D., Abubakari the Second, ruler of the northwest African kingdom of Mali, sent ships to the west looking for a new land. A year later one of the ships returned, the frightened captain turning around before going too far, leaving the rest of the fleet to go on alone. Undaunted, Abubakari assembled a fleet of ships along with the kingdom's best seamen and navigators. He would lead the next expedition himself. He turned the kingdom over to his brother and set sail. We know for certain that he left, and the fact that his name is never mentioned again is more fuel for the flame.

The speculation regarding visitors to the New World from Africa centers around huge basalt boulders on which are carved likenesses with unmistakable negroid features. They were found enmeshed in undergrowth in Mesoamerican jungles. Would an artist of that or any other age go to the effort involved in carving a six-foot high likeness for fun? And is it a true likeness of a leader or deity, or a stylized version peculiar to that time and place? Scholars point out that it is not a portrait of a negro because some of the natives of the area today have the same flat nose and thick-lipped profile. In rejoinder, of course, they are asked to explain where the native profiles came from. Although the carved heads are believed to be much older than Abubakari's voyage, the good King's travels are pointed to as an example of the possibilities.

Just as common, or more so, are the startling parallels many of the same people draw between the Egyptian culture and the Aztec and Mayans. Did east influence west, or is it a case of coincidental evolution as the official line says?

Unless someone translates some long lost manuscript or unearths some conclusive bit of evidence on these shores, the questions of who arrived in America first and whether or not there were outside influences on the indigenous population of the Americas will probably never be answered. Easier to answer, if we only knew where to look, is the question of how long man has been in the Western Hemisphere.

The most thoroughly documented theory is the one presented in this book: that Mongol hunters crossed the Bering land bridge and over a period of many years, even centuries, moved south and east until man was in every corner of the continent where he could make a living. According to this widely accepted theory, man has been in the Americas about 40,000 years. As usual, however, there are those who keep throwing flies in the ointment of scholarship.

An announcement of an astonishing find in Brazil was made in 1982. Maria Beltrao, digging in a remote section of the northeastern backlands near Central, Brazil has found bones so old that they could not be dated by the Carbon 14 dating method, which can measure back about 40,000 years. According to the Center of Weak Radiation of the National Scientific Research Center in Gif-Sur-Yvette, France, the bones, which are from an extinct specie of horse and had been broken and bore marks that could have been caused by a chopper, were dated at over 350,000 years old. The French are ninety per cent sure of the number. Along with the horse bones were found the teeth of a giant peccary and a pebble tool, or chopper, the most primitive of tools used by man. The bone deposits were uncovered when a drought dried up the massive stone cisterns that serve as community wells in the town of Central.

In nearby Xique-Xique, a cave called Grotto of the Cosmos houses paintings of suns, stars and comets. In the low light of the cave, a red comet 4½ feet long soars across the low ceiling against a backdrop of painted stars. Red suns rise and set amidst figures of lizards, a traditional companion to the sun. An imposing drawing of red and black concentric circles surrounded by spokes could be an illustration of a supernova, according to Ronaldo Mourao, director of the Museum of Astronomy in Rio de Janeiro.

Near the entrance is a notch where every year, exactly on the winter solstice (June 21 south of the equator) sunlight streams through, illuminating a red sun painted on the slanted ceiling. The delicate alignment through the rock is not unlike a find in Canyon de Chelly in New Mexico, except that Mourao claims the Grotto of the Cosmos is much older, possibly the oldest astronomical observatory in the world.

Who were the hunters and who were the astronomers? Were they the same people? If the dates from France are correct, the bones were the product of kills not by Cro-Magnon man but by Neanderthal man. But the prevailing wisdom is that Neanderthal man was not in the Western Hemisphere at all. In fact, according to the accepted land bridge theory, no one was here before 40,000 years ago.

Several explanations are possible. Perhaps Neanderthals migrated to the Americas and died out before the Cro-Magnon came. Maybe it is a case of true coincidental evolution. That is, since similar conditions existed in the Americas as in the rest of the world, why couldn't man evolve in a similar manner in the Western Hemisphere as he did in the East? Or maybe we are looking at evidence left by a heretofore unknown, and extinct, kind of man. Then again, maybe it was Neanderthal. The more scholars find out about Neanderthal, the more complex he becomes. We know, for instance, that primative Neanderthals used flowers to decorate graves in the caves of France. Perhaps he could also build a boat and get here of his own accord. Or maybe none of these theories or explanations will replace the well-documented land bridge theory.

It is certain, though, that the only way we will ever know when the first man walked the land in the Americas is through rational and persistent research into the records that lay buried beneath our feet.

APPENDIX

A Note on the Illustrated Narratives

PREHISTORY

The presentation is fiction. The manner in which the Coahuiltecans react to different situations in the story is based on historical accounts, so far as they go, and conjecture based on the known reactions of similar peoples. The events that take place are based on archaeological reports, in particular the burial. The bones of a young female, 15 to 16 years old, were found with the bones of a fetus in the abdominal area. In her lap rested a partial skeleton of a male approximately forty years old. This find, in Cameron County at the Floyd Morris site was burial 11 and is reported in detail by Thomas R. Hester in *Digging into South Texas Prehistory*. I took the liberty of moving the site a hundred miles west to fit the story. I have always been intrigued by what might have been the reactions of the Indians who first saw a horse's hoof print without benefit of seeing its maker.

MISSIONS

The facts can be found in books pertaining to the missions of Texas listed in the bibliography, including the story of one missionary who carried a life-sized statue of St. Anthony from Saltillo into the wilderness of Texas on the back of a donkey. Most of the missions in Texas began in the same manner. A missionary, either at the church's initiative or at the request of a specific group of Indians, would find a suitable spot for the complex and, with a military guard and Indian labor, would construct a mission. The missions were charged with converting the savages. The church would then be turned over to a parish priest, allowing the missionary to go on to other challenges. Ideally, a town would grow up around the church. Readers familiar with San José Mission in San Antonio might note the similarity with the drawing of the mission in the story, although it is not meant to represent San José itself.

CADDO

This segment is based entirely upon information gleaned from *The Indians of Texas* by W. W. Newcomb.

TONKAWA

The story is fictitious although the demeanor and physical appearance of the Tonkawa and their environment is based on various sources. The story points out that as the couple's life is just beginning, the Indian's existence is ending.

KARANKAWA

This is a highlight history of the tribe based on historic record. The physical appearance of the Indians and their land is supported by contemporary sources, as is the costuming of the Anglo-Americans, the Spaniards, and the weaponry. The grandmother figure is a device to make the story easier to read and is not based on any known individual, although one may have existed.

DELAWARE

This narrative shows the interaction between the Anglo-Americans and the Delawares, most of whom, unlike the Comanches, tried to assimilate into the white man's world. The Delaware segment is based on historic record. A famous Delaware scout named Jim Shaw is the subject of a short biography in *The Handbook of Texas*, and mention of him comes up in many pioneer narratives of the times. He was active on the frontier from 1841 to 1858, when he was killed in a fall from the roof of a house he was building for himself. Despite being described as "a handsome man of superior intelligence" Jim Shaw was not related to the author.

COMANCHES

The story is a consolidation of many contemporary accounts, all written by white men. In this instance, I have related a short history of the Comanches and, drawing upon the accounts, have told the story of a typical raid at the twilight of the tribe's power.

BIBLIOGRAPHY

Bannon, John F. *The Spanish Borderlands Frontier, 1513–1821*. 1970. Reprint. Albuquerque: University of New Mexico Press, 1980.

Boyd, Maurice. *Kiowa Voices, Myths, Legends and Folktales*. Volume II. Fort Worth: Texas Christian University Press, 1983.

Branda, Eldon S., ed. *The Handbook of Texas: A Supplement*. Volume III. Austin: The Texas State Historical Association, 1976.

Canty, Carol Shannon. New World Pastoralism: A Study of the Comanche Indians. Master's thesis, University of Texas at San Antonio, 1986.

Catlin, George. *Letters and Notes on the Manners, Customs and Conditions of North American Indians*. Volumes 1 and 2. 1841. Reprint. New York: Dover Publications Inc., 1973.

Cisneros, Jose. *Riders Across the Centuries: Horseman of the Spanish Borderlands*. El Paso: Texas Western Press, 1984.

Coe, Michael, D. Snow and E. Benson. *Atlas of Ancient America*. New York: Facts on File Publications, Inc., 1986.

Davis, John L. *Exploration in Texas Ancient and Otherwise*. San Antonio: Institute of Texan Cultures, 1984.

Dixon, Olive K. *Life of "Billy" Dixon: Plainsman, Scout and Pioneer*. 1927. Reprint. Austin: State House Press, 1986.

Fehrenbach, T.R. *Comanches: The Destruction of a People*. New York: Alfred A. Knopf, 1974.

Foster, Nancy H. *The Alamo and Other Texas Missions to Remember*. Houston: Lone Star Books, 1984.

Fox, Daniel E. *Traces of Texas History*. San Antonio: Corona Publishing Co., 1983.

Haley, James L. *Texas, An Album of History*. New York: Doubleday and Co., 1985.

Haynes, Michaele T. Alterations in Delaware Personal Appearance as an Indication of Acculturation. Master's thesis, University of Texas at San Antonio, 1985.